best ever

 low fat

p

This is a Parragon Book
First published in 2003

Parragon
Queen Street House
4 Queen Street
Bath BA1 1HE
United Kingdom

Created and produced by
The Bridgewater Book Company Ltd,
Lewes, East Sussex

Photographer Ian Parsons

ISBN: 1–40540-522-8

Printed in China

NOTE

This book uses metric and imperial measurements. Follow the same
units of measurement throughout; do not mix metric and imperial. All spoon
measurements are level: teaspoons are assumed to be 5 ml and tablespoons are
assumed to be 15 ml. Unless otherwise stated, milk is assumed to be full fat,
eggs and individual vegetables such as potatoes are medium, and pepper is
freshly ground black pepper.

The times given for each recipe are an approximate guide only.
The preparation times may differ according to the techniques used by different
people and the cooking times may vary as a result of the type of oven used.
Ovens should be preheated to the specified temperature. If using a fan-assisted
oven, check the manufacturer's instructions for adjusting the time and temperature.
The preparation times include chilling and marinating times, where appropriate.

The nutritional information provided for each recipe is per serving or per
portion. Optional ingredients, variations or serving suggestions have not been
included in the calculations.

Recipes using raw or very lightly cooked eggs should be avoided
by infants, the elderly, pregnant women, convalescents and anyone
suffering from an illness.

contents

introduction

As we are becoming more aware of how we can improve our own and our family's health, low-fat cooking is becoming increasingly popular. However, low-fat food is often wrongly perceived as being 'diet' food and, therefore, boring, bland and unappetizing. This is simply not true and this book will help to change any misconceptions. Low-fat cooking is healthier and often less expensive, and there is a huge variety of tasty dishes.

From day-to-day family suppers to sophisticated dinner parties, this book is packed with delicious recipe ideas and tips. You will find many family favourites in the following pages, such as Easy Gazpacho (see page 22), Pasta with Low-fat Pesto (see page 58), Meatballs with Tomato Relish (see page 116) and Smoked Haddock Pie (see page 176). There is even a selection of low-fat sandwich fillings for quick and easy snacks.

While nutritionists and health professionals agree that most people in the Western world eat too much fat, this does not mean that you should try to cut it out of your diet completely. Everybody needs to consume a certain amount of fat for general health and well-being. Fats are a concentrated source of energy and provide valuable vitamins. Essential fats are – as their name suggests – essential. The type of fat consumed is as important as the quantity (see page 6). However, as a rule, your daily intake of fats should not exceed more than 30 per cent of the day's total average of 2,000 calories (for adults). As each gram of fat provides nine calories, simple arithmetic shows that the average daily intake of fat should be no more than 66.7 g (2½ oz).

Some people can eat nothing but burgers and fries and still stay slim, but this does not mean that they are healthy. By doing more exercise and having a higher metabolic rate, you can burn off more of the fat you have consumed, but you will not be so healthy as your friend who consumes less fat and exercises moderately. Whether you want to lose weight, have been told to eat less fat by your doctor or simply want to improve your family's health, use this book to guide you to a healthier and happier lifestyle. This book also includes tips on how to choose lower-fat ingredients in place of the butter, cream, cheese and red meats to which we have all become accustomed, as well as advice on healthy cooking techniques and useful equipment.

changing your eating patterns

Food is always more appetizing if it is presented attractively. All of the recipes in this book use colour and style, as well as flavour and texture, to make your meal thoroughly enjoyable. If you are entertaining guests, why not try one of the following combinations? For vegetarian guests, serve Lentil & Tomato Soup (see page 25), followed by Roast Summer Vegetables (see page 72) and Lemon Granita (see page 229). Serve Parma Ham with Figs (see page 49), Beef in Beer (see page 117) and Hot Chocolate Cherries (see page 220) as a winter meal for meat-lovers. Chicken & Asparagus Timbales (see page 44), followed by Lamb Tagine (see page 134) and Peach Sorbet (see page 230), is an ideal meal for a dinner party.

The recipes featured in this book are just a few of the many delicious low-fat meals you can make. They vary in difficulty from quick and easy to more time-consuming and skilful. Many of the dishes are also suitable for freezing and re-heating in an oven or microwave. You can even take them to work and heat them up at lunchtime, leaving no excuses for indulging in takeaways.

types of fat

Keeping track of which fats to eat and which to avoid, counting calories and keeping a wary eye on sugar and salt content can all seem overwhelming. The thing to remember is that too many saturated fats are harmful, but unsaturated fats in moderation are beneficial.

You will find saturated fats in foods such as red meat, butter, hard cheese (like Cheddar), biscuits, cakes, pastries and chocolate. Although they are mostly found in animal products, there are some vegetable sources too. Coconut and palm oil are both high in saturated fats, as are most fats that are solid at room temperature.

There are two different types of unsaturated fats – monounsaturated and polyunsaturated. Monounsaturated fats are better for you than saturated fats, but are not so good as polyunsaturated fats. Monounsaturated fats are found in olive oil, rapeseed oil, nuts, seeds, oily fish and avocados. These are fine if consumed in moderate quantities and are thought to reduce cholesterol level in the blood. This may explain why there is a low incidence of heart disease in some Mediterranean countries where olive oil, avocados and oily fish are eaten regularly.

The body needs polyunsaturated fats for various functions. Both omega-3 and omega-6 fatty acids are classed by nutritionists as essential. Omega-3 fatty acids are needed for healthy cells and brain development. Polyunsaturated fats help to protect against heart disease, arthritis and some other medical conditions. Polyunsaturated fats are found in fish oils, oily fish, walnuts, olive oil and sunflower oil. They are usually liquid at room temperature.

Be careful of processed oils labelled 'hydrogenated vegetable oils', as some of the good unsaturated fats are converted to unhealthy saturated fats – or trans fats – by the process used to make them.

cholesterol

Raised cholesterol levels in the blood are regarded as a cause for concern, as levels that are constantly high or rising are thought to cause heart disease. The best way to avoid this happening is to eat a varied and balanced diet. Cut out, or at least cut down on, foods such as solid cooking fats (lard and hard margarine), biscuits, cakes, pastries, chocolate, fatty meat, processed foods (including sausages), and full-fat dairy products (butter, cream and hard cheeses). Medical research shows that if you cut down to almost no saturated fats, you may be able to reduce your blood cholesterol level by more than 10 per cent. Foods thought to be helpful in reducing blood cholesterol levels include wholemeal bread, Granary bread, cereal containing cooked bran, rolled oats, oranges, apples, bananas, figs, prunes, sweetcorn, garlic, onions, red kidney beans and other pulses. Try having Fruity Flapjacks (see page 253) as a low-cholesterol alternative to cakes.

a balanced diet

There are five main food groups, and you should try to eat a certain amount from each group daily. The first group consists of fruit and vegetables (not potatoes), and provides you mainly with vitamins and minerals. The advice is to eat at least five portions from this group per day and that at least some of them should be uncooked. This may sound like a lot, but you will be able to eat the daily recommendation if you spread it throughout the day – for example, choose a banana and cereal for breakfast, a sandwich with salad for lunch and steamed chicken with broccoli, carrots and peas for dinner. Try to snack on healthy alternatives to crisps and chocolate, such as fruit.

The second group includes staples such as rice, pasta, bread, potatoes and cereals. These contain complex carbohydrates, which release energy at a steady rate, and dietary fibre, which aids digestion. It is recommended that we try to consume several servings of these foods each day. Having a rice salad (with a low-fat dressing) for lunch, potatoes with dinner and Fat-free Marble Cake (see page 248) for dessert will be an adequate intake for most people. This group helps to keep your digestive system working efficiently and is thought to help reduce the chances of stomach and bowel cancers.

The third food group is the protein foods – meat, fish and poultry. Red meat can be high in saturated fats and you need to trim off any visible fat before cooking. Poultry and fish are the healthiest ingredients. Eat plenty of oily fish, such as sardines, mackerel, tuna, salmon and herrings, as they are rich in omega-3 essential fatty acids. You do not need to eat foods from this group every day if you have a mixed diet. When you do eat them, you need only small quantities. About 25 per cent of the fat we consume comes from meat and meat products. Even trimmed meats, such as lamb chops, pork loin and fillet steak, can contain high amounts of fats. Vegetarians can sometimes have an inadequate intake of protein. They should take care to eat a varied diet that includes tofu and other vegetable proteins.

The fourth food group is made up of dairy products, including milk, cheese and cream. You need a moderate amount of these foods daily. Growing children, pregnant women and the elderly, especially those suffering from a bone disease such as osteoporosis, require a higher intake of calcium and should adjust their diets accordingly. Most dairy products contain a very high proportion of fats, and eating large amounts can make it more difficult to lose weight or keep blood cholesterol levels down. About 20 per cent of the fat we consume comes from this food group.

Be careful about the fifth food group. It consists of foods that contain fat and sugar, such as margarine, chocolate and sweet pastries. You need only very small amounts of food from this group as you will obtain the small intake of fat you require from other food groups.

Being aware of hidden fats is important. It is easy to cut down on fatty foods, but knowing where to look for the real low-fat alternatives is essential. Many nuts and seeds are rich in essential fatty acids, but also have quite a high overall fat content. Even trimmed 'lean' meat can contain up to 10 per cent fat.

A varied diet is a healthy diet, and you should aim to eat different foods each day, as they all have different combinations and quantities of nutrients. Try different types of pasta, such as Fettuccine with Smoked Salmon (see page 60) and Rigatoni with Squid (see page 204). When cooking pasta, resist the temptation to add a few drops of oil to the saucepan to prevent it sticking, as this raises the fat content. Making use of exotic fruits and vegetables will also make a low-fat diet more interesting.

low-fat cooking techniques

You may be used to putting a knob of butter or lard into the frying pan before adding the streaky bacon – this doesn't mean that you should. Instead of adding the saturated fat, try grilling without any added fat. Instead of streaky, try lean bacon and trim off any visible fat. You could even get rid of the bacon altogether. Knowing what the alternatives are is the key to enjoying your new low-fat diet. You don't have to forego everything you enjoy eating. Sitting down to a family meal together can be one of the most pleasurable parts of your day.

It is worthwhile investing in good-quality, non-stick cookware. Cast iron, stainless steel and heavy-gauge aluminium are ideal and you will find that you need very little fat, as the heat is evenly distributed. If you need to add fat, use oils high in unsaturated fats, such as olive or sunflower oil. Cans of 'spray oils' are even more effective at minimizing the amount you use, as you can give the saucepan a light, even coat.

As a rule, avoid frying, as it is the least healthy way of cooking. Stir-frying is better as long as you use very little oil. Use a good-quality wok and keep the temperature high, tossing the ingredients constantly so that they do not stick. Try Prawn Stir-fry (see page 206). The best advice about deep-frying is: don't!

Vegetables can be cooked in many ways and are often especially healthy when eaten raw. Try cooking them in juice, stock and/or wine for a tasty alternative to oil. Steamed vegetables have a more vibrant colour, firmer texture and retain more nutrients than boiled vegetables. Boiling vegetables is a no-fat way of cooking, but it also destroys many of their nutrients, especially vitamins. Try microwaving as a quick alternative to boiling or steaming.

Grilling is one of the healthiest methods of cooking and a number of foods can be cooked this way. Thread diced chicken and vegetables on to skewers, then barbecue or grill as kebabs. Barbecuing imparts a beautiful flavour to the food and is healthy, although be careful to eat vegetables to balance the protein. Try not to burn barbecue food, as this is not only unappetizing, but is also believed to be carcinogenic (cancer-causing).

Griddling in a ridged griddle pan is a healthy compromise between shallow-frying and grilling. The food cooks rapidly and if oil is needed, lightly brushing over the griddle pan is all that is required. If poached chicken seems like boiled meat to you, try poaching chicken breasts in stock with white wine and herbs. You do not need to use any oil and can steam vegetables over the saucepan while the meat is cooking. Poaching is also ideal for fish.

Instead of adding flavourings as you cook, you can use a marinade. Meat and poultry are made tender by marinating overnight or for at least 4 hours in a mixture of lemon juice, oil, herbs, garlic and either vinegar or alcohol. Do not marinate fish for longer than 1 hour.

When you are baking desserts, use good-quality bakeware. Use greaseproof paper or baking paper to eliminate the need to coat the cake tins in butter before adding the mixture. A light brushing of oil is sufficient.

from high fat to low fat

When buying meat, ask your butcher to trim off any visible fat or to remove the bone so that you can easily trim the meat. If you shop in a supermarket, it is not easy to see what you are buying if it is pre-packed. Buy from the delicatessen or butcher and do not be afraid to ask him to put a piece back and get you another.

Many supermarkets now stock an extensive range of low-fat and low-calorie products, such as milk, cheese, yogurt, salad dressings, crisps and biscuits. However, even if the label says 'low fat', it is still best to have a look at the ingredients list. Avoid products labelled 'reduced fat', as they may have a very high saturated fat content.

Low-fat spreads are available in every shop and supermarket and it can be confusing to read all the labels, which make various claims. Generally, some are only for spreading and others are only for cooking. Olive oil provides the best flavour when cooking, but can be expensive to use regularly. For spreading, you can buy the very low-fat spreads, but these have a high water content and are not suitable for cooking. Spreads labelled low-fat or half-fat are suitable for spreading and baking and have a fat content of about 40 per cent, compared with the very low-fat spreads with about 20 per cent.

Gradually changing and enhancing your diet is far better and safer than suddenly stopping eating one thing and switching to another. There are many ways to re-adjust your diet and that of your family without extra financial cost or effort in the kitchen.

To begin with, eat less of the foods that contain lots of saturated fats. Buy low-fat spreads and olive oil or polyunsaturated oils for cooking.

Limit fatty meats, such as lamb and pork, to occasional treats and eat chicken, turkey, fish and venison instead. Trim any visible fat from the meat and remove the skin. If you are fond of a roast dinner, try putting a chicken on a rack with a roasting tin underneath. Cover it with herbs and garlic and baste occasionally with stock – cook at the same temperature and for the same length of time as a normal roast. Instead of making gravy the traditional way, try reducing stock or vegetable cooking water and freezing it in meal-size portions, then thicken with cornflour and add salt, pepper and herbs.

Instead of basing meals around meat, try a meal based around eggs, such as Mexican Eggs (see page 74), or around vegetables, such as Layered Vegetable Bake (see page 88). Sausages can be high in saturated fats – choose low-fat varieties or make your own. Prick them with a fork so that the fat can run out, place on a rack and grill.

Even if you are not a vegetarian, use tofu in place of meat sometimes for a healthy, low-fat alternative. Try Vegetable & Tofu Stir-fry (see page 152).

Full-fat dairy products can raise blood cholesterol levels and contribute to obesity. This is a high risk for vegetarians, who often rely too heavily on cheese for protein. Avoid these full-fat products altogether and switch to semi-skimmed or skimmed milk products, which will make a huge difference to your fat intake.

Low-fat yogurts are readily available in almost all food shops and are a great idea for a healthy lunch. Buy low-fat natural yogurt and use it as a substitute for cream to thicken sauces and add to desserts. A bowl of low-fat natural yogurt with honey or jam (which contain no fat at all) makes a healthy and delicious start to the day. Low-fat and no-fat fromage frais are also healthy options which can be used in both sweet and savoury dishes.

Instead of buying French fries and crisps, look for low-fat crackers, breadsticks and savoury biscuits. If you cannot find any, you can make your own by baking thin slices of potato coated with herbs and spices. Most supermarkets now have a range of very low-fat crisps, most of them baked with little or no oil. If you eat out and find that everything is served with chips, ask if they have baked potatoes, rice or pasta.

Avoid eating cakes, biscuits, chocolate, tortilla chips and pastries and resist vending machines and canteens at work. If you find a health food shop too inconvenient, make your own snacks. Fresh fruit and vegetables are the best things to snack on. Dried fruits, such as apricots, figs, prunes and raisins, are also a healthier option, although high in sugar. Try slices of carrot, pieces of cauliflower, spring onion, radishes, cucumber or hard-boiled eggs with a dip, such as low-fat hummus, natural yogurt with herbs or ready-made low-fat dips.

Slices of apple dipped in honey can be a delicious quick snack if you have a sweet tooth. Sorbets, such as Peach Sorbet (see page 230), make a good low-fat alternative to ice cream and are just as delicious on a hot summer's day. You can make muesli bars using rolled oats, and bran muffins and biscuits using low-fat ingredients. Instead of chocolate toppings, try making a yogurt topping. Canned fruit is also a good option, although you should avoid fruits that are preserved in syrup. Although there is no fat in syrup, the sugar content is high and natural fruit juice is better.

If you regularly eat takeaways, this is one of the first things to address. Almost everything seems to be deep-fried in saturated fats and is bad for your cholesterol levels, your weight and your heart. Try home-made burgers and you will discover a new taste experience, as well as cutting down your fat intake. Takeaway pizza is high in saturated fats and the best thing you can do is make your own at home. If you do end up getting a takeaway pizza, blot each slice well with kitchen paper to soak up excess fat on the surface. You can adapt all sorts of traditional and favourite meals to a low-fat diet, just as you can adapt them for a diabetic, vegetarian or low-sodium diet.

the low-fat family

Exercise is as important as eating healthily and nobody really has any excuse for not doing some exercise. Walking is one of the best ways to burn off extra fat and calories, and aids digestion. Moderate exercise a little while after a meal is safe, but you shouldn't begin a heavy workout soon after eating or you will give yourself indigestion. If you are trying to involve your whole family in a lifestyle change, go for walks together after a low-fat

lunch. A picnic is the ideal setting for a low-fat meal and many recipes in this book are easy to make, pack up and carry. Ideas for picnic nibbles include Trout Mousse (see page 52) with low-fat crackers or breadsticks, or Crudités with Garlic Chive & Coriander Dip (see page 38). Persuading the family to eat a low-fat diet with you can be difficult. If part of your aim is to lose weight, point out all the benefits to your family.

Be careful about putting children on diets. If your child is overweight, consult your doctor before making any drastic changes in their diet. Children need different amounts of nutrients and are very sensitive to changes in lifestyle. Cutting down on crisps, chocolate, sweets, fast food and fatty snacks is the first step and this can be done without seeing a doctor first. Children under five years old should not be given skimmed or semi-skimmed milk or dairy products made from them.

Children will invariably complain about eating vegetables, but if you serve them in an attractive way, perhaps with a dressing, you are more likely to get a positive response. Snacks for children could include breadsticks and dips, home-made crisps, fruit slices, and fruit kebabs dipped in honey and grilled (on skewers without sharp points), and home-made low-fat ice cream. Many of these things are a good idea for healthy packed lunches to take to school. Try Scrumptious Sandwiches (see page 62), Vegetable Samosas (see page 86) and Spicy Chicken with Naan (see page 66) – with a little less spice for very young ones.

Many people are very wary of low-fat 'diets', yet they often pay little attention to how their evening meal is prepared. If your family is used to steak, egg and chips smothered in ketchup, serve grilled steak with the fat trimmed off, baked potato with low-fat spread, steamed vegetables or salad and home-made low-fat mayonnaise or tomato chutney. You do not need to tell them that the meal is low-fat – simply serve it up and wait for their requests for a second helping!

basic recipes

vegetable stock

makes: 2 litres/3½ pints
preparation time: 10 minutes
cooking time: 40 minutes

2 tbsp sunflower oil
115 g/4 oz onions, finely chopped
115 g/4 oz leeks, finely chopped
115 g/4 oz carrots, finely chopped
4 celery sticks, finely chopped
85 g/3 oz fennel, finely chopped
85 g/3 oz tomatoes, finely chopped
2.25 litres/4 pints water
1 bouquet garni

1 Heat the oil in a large saucepan. Add the onions and leeks and cook over a low heat, stirring occasionally, for 5 minutes, or until softened.

2 Add the remaining vegetables, cover and cook over a low heat, stirring occasionally, for 10 minutes. Add the water and bouquet garni, bring to the boil and simmer for 20 minutes.

3 Sieve, cool and store in the refrigerator. Use immediately or freeze in portions for up to 3 months.

cook's tip

To make the bouquet garni, tie 4 fresh parsley stems, 1 clove, 1 bay leaf and 4 peppercorns in a piece of clean muslin.

fish stock

makes: 1.3 litres/2¼ pints
preparation time: 10 minutes
cooking time: 30 minutes

650 g/1 lb 7 oz white fish heads, bones and trimmings, rinsed
1 onion, sliced
2 celery sticks, chopped
1 carrot, sliced
1 bay leaf
4 fresh parsley sprigs
4 black peppercorns
½ lemon, sliced

1.3 litres/2¼ pints water
125 ml/4 fl oz dry white wine

1 Place the fish heads, bones and trimmings in a large saucepan. Add the remaining ingredients, then bring to the boil and skim off the foam that rises to the surface with a slotted spoon.

2 Reduce the heat, partially cover and simmer gently for 25 minutes.

3 Sieve the stock, without pressing down on the contents of the sieve. Cool and store in the refrigerator. Use immediately or freeze in portions for up to 3 months.

variation

Shellfish stock has a beautifully delicate flavour. Use prawn heads and shells with white fish trimmings.

chicken stock

makes: 2.5 litres/4½ pints
preparation time: 15 minutes, plus 30 minutes chilling
cooking time: 3½ hours

1.3 kg/3 lb chicken wings and necks
2 onions, cut into wedges
4 litres/7 pints water
2 carrots, roughly chopped
2 celery sticks, roughly chopped
10 fresh parsley sprigs
4 fresh thyme sprigs
2 bay leaves
10 black peppercorns

1 Place the chicken wings and necks and the onions in a large, heavy-based saucepan and cook over a low heat, stirring frequently, until browned all over.

2 Add the water and stir to scrape off sediment on the base of the pan. Bring to the boil and skim off any foam. Add the remaining ingredients, partially cover and simmer gently for 3 hours.

3 Sieve, cool and chill in the refrigerator. When cold, carefully remove and discard the layer of fat that has set on the surface. Use immediately or freeze in portions for up to 6 months.

beef stock

makes: 1.7 litres/3 pints
preparation time: 15 minutes, plus 30 minutes chilling
cooking time: 4¼ hours

1 kg/2 lb 4 oz beef marrow bones, sawn into 7.5-cm/3-inch pieces
650 g/1 lb 7 oz stewing beef in 1 piece
2.8 litres/5 pints water
4 cloves
2 onions, halved
2 celery sticks, roughly chopped
8 peppercorns
1 bouquet garni

1 Place the bones in the base of a large, heavy-based saucepan and put the beef on top. Add the water and bring to the boil over a low heat, skimming off all the foam that rises to the surface.

2 Press a clove into each onion half and add to the saucepan with the celery, peppercorns and bouquet garni. Reduce the heat, partially cover and simmer very gently for 3 hours. Remove the meat and simmer for a further 1 hour.

3 Sieve, cool and chill in the refrigerator. When cold, carefully remove and discard the layer of fat that has set on the surface. Use immediately or freeze in portions for up to 6 months.

low-fat mayonnaise

makes: 200 ml/7 fl oz
preparation time: 10 minutes,
plus 10 minutes standing
cooking time: 0 minutes

4 hard-boiled egg yolks
2 tbsp white wine vinegar
2 tbsp lemon juice
1 tsp Dijon mustard
salt and pepper
4 tbsp low-fat natural yogurt

1 Mix the egg yolks, vinegar, lemon juice and mustard together, then season to taste with salt and pepper. Mash thoroughly with a fork to blend.

2 Beat in the yogurt, 1 tablespoon at a time, until incorporated.

3 Cover with clingfilm and leave to stand for 10 minutes to allow the flavours to mingle.

saffron sauce

serves: 6
preparation time: 15 minutes
cooking time: 0 minutes

1 egg yolk
pinch of salt
pinch of powdered saffron
¼ tsp ground coriander
¼ tsp ground cumin
150 ml/5 fl oz sunflower oil
1½ tsp white wine vinegar
1½ tsp lemon juice
150 ml/5 fl oz low-fat natural yogurt

1 Put the egg yolk in a bowl and beat with the salt, then stir in the saffron, coriander and cumin.

2 Add the sunflower oil, one drop at a time, beating constantly. When half the oil has been incorporated, add the remainder in a steady stream, beating constantly.

3 Stir in the vinegar and lemon juice and fold in the yogurt. Cover and chill in the refrigerator until required.

cook's tip

For a quick and easy low-fat dressing, put 1 tablespoon of clear honey in a bowl, add 6 tablespoons of low-fat natural yogurt and beat until blended. Season to taste.

Fat content of common foods

The following figures show the weight of fat in grams per 100 g/3½ oz of each food.

vegetables

Aubergine	0.4 g
Beetroot, raw	0.1 g
Broccoli	0.9 g
Cabbage	0.4 g
Carrots	0.3 g
Cauliflower	0.9 g
Celery	0.2 g
Chips, home-made	6.7 g
Chips, oven	4.2 g
Chips, ready-made	12.4 g
Courgettes	0.4 g
Cucumber	0.1 g
Mushrooms	0.5 g
Onions	0.2 g
Peas	1.5 g
Potatoes	0.2 g
Tomatoes	0.3 g

pulses

Black-eyed beans, cooked	1.8 g
Butter beans, canned	0.5 g
Chickpeas, canned	2.9 g
Hummus	12.6 g
Red kidney beans, canned	0.6 g
Red lentils, cooked	0.4 g

fish and shellfish

Cod fillets, raw	0.7 g
Crab, canned	0.5 g
Crab, cooked	2.0 g
Haddock, raw	0.6 g
Lemon sole, raw	1.5 g
Mussels	2.0 g
Prawns	0.9 g
Trout, grilled	5.4 g
Tuna, canned in brine	0.6 g
Tuna, canned in oil	9.0 g

meat

Bacon, streaky	39.5 g
Beef, minced, raw	16.2 g
Beef, minced, extra lean, raw	9.6 g
Rump steak, trimmed, raw	4.1 g
Lamb, trimmed, raw	8.3 g
Pork, trimmed, raw	4.0 g
Chicken breast portion, raw	1.1 g
Chicken, roasted	12.5 g
Duck, meat only, raw	6.5 g
Duck, roasted	38.1 g
Turkey, meat only, raw	1.6 g

dairy and fats

Brie	26.9 g
Butter	81.7 g
Cheddar	34.4 g
Cheddar, reduced-fat	15.0 g
Cream cheese	47.4 g
Cream, double	48.0 g
Cream, double, reduced fat	24.0 g
Cream, single	19.1 g
Cream, whipping	39.3 g
Crème fraîche	40.0 g
Crème fraîche, reduced-fat	15.0 g
Edam	25.4 g
Feta	20.2 g
Fromage frais	7.1 g
Fromage frais, very low-fat	0.2 g
Lard	99.0 g
Low-fat spread	40.5 g
Low-fat spread, very	25.0 g
Margarine	81.6 g
Milk, full-fat	3.9 g
Milk, skimmed	0.1 g
Parmesan	32.7 g
Skimmed milk soft cheese	trace
Yogurt, low-fat	0.8 g
Yogurt, Greek	9.1 g
Yogurt, reduced-fat, Greek	5.0 g

oils

Corn oil	99.9 g
Olive oil	99.9 g
Safflower oil	99.9 g

eggs

Whole egg	10.8 g
Egg yolk	30.5 g
Egg white	trace

dressings

Fat-free dressing	1.2 g
Mayonnaise	75.6 g
Mayonnaise, reduced calorie	28.1 g
Vinaigrette	49.4 g

cereals and baking

Bread, brown	2.0 g
Bread, white	1.9 g
Bread, wholemeal	2.5 g
Chocolate, milk	30.7 g
Chocolate, plain	28.0 g
Cornflakes	0.7 g
Croissants	20.3 g
Digestive biscuits	20.9 g
Digestive biscuits, reduced-fat	16.4 g
Doughnut, jam	14.5 g
Sponge cake, fat-free	6.1 g
Flapjack	26.6 g
Flour, white	1.3 g
Flour, wholemeal	2.2 g
Madeira cake	16.9 g
Muesli	5.9 g
Naan bread	12.5 g
Pasta, white, uncooked	1.8 g
Pasta, wholemeal, uncooked	2.5 g
Pitta bread	1.2 g
Rice, brown, uncooked	2.8 g
Rice, white, uncooked	3.6 g
Shortbread	26.1 g
Sugar, white	0.3 g
Sultana bran	1.6 g

preserves

Honey	0 g
Jam	0.26 g
Lemon curd	5.0 g

processed foods

Baked beans in tomato sauce	0.6 g
Burger, grilled	14.0 g
Burger, fried	17.0 g
Fish fingers	12.0 g
Pork pie	27.0 g
Salami	45.2 g
Sausages	22.0 g
Sausages, low-fat	6.0 g
Sausage roll	36.4 g

fruit

Apples, eating	0.1 g
Apricots	0.1 g
Avocados	19.5 g
Bananas	0.3 g
Cherries	0.1 g
Currants, black/red/white	1.0 g
Dried mixed fruit	0.4 g
Grapefruit	0.1 g
Olives, in brine	11.0 g
Oranges	0.1 g
Peaches	0.1 g
Pears	0.1 g
Prunes	0.2 g

nuts

Almonds	55.8 g
Brazil nuts	68.2 g
Hazelnuts	63.5 g
Peanuts, plain	46.1 g
Peanut butter	53.7 g
Pine kernels	68.6 g
Walnuts	68.5 g

soups & appetizers

Few things are simpler and more delicious than home-made soup. The recipes here range from winter warmers for family suppers to chilled summer soup, as well as delicately flavoured elegant soups to grace a dinner party table. The secret of success lies in using a well-made, flavoursome stock. An added advantage of home-made stock (see page 11) is that you have total control over what goes into it and you can be sure to skim off every last trace of fat from the surface once it has been chilled. You can, of course, use stock cubes or bouillon powder, but do read the labels carefully before buying and try to find a brand that is not too salty.

The starters featured in this chapter include a mouthwatering selection of vegetarian specialities, as well as delicious dishes with fish, shellfish, chicken and Parma ham – and most of them with fewer than 10 g (¼ oz) of fat per serving. Some require no cooking at all and can be assembled in moments, while others are more elaborate and extravagant dishes for special occasions. There are tempting treats for every time of year, from wonderful ways with summery asparagus (see pages 44 and 48) to the spectacular Oysters Rockefeller (see page 55) for when there's an 'r' in the month, as well as any-time dishes, from easy Antipasto Mushrooms (see page 35) to sophisticated Trout Mousse (see page 52).

consommé

serves 4   **prep: 15 mins, plus** ⌛ **1 hr standing**   **cook: 1 hr 15 mins** ⏲

A traditional clear soup made from beef bones and lean beef. Thin strips of vegetables provide a colourful garnish and if served with Melba toast it makes the perfect start to any dinner party.

INGREDIENTS

1.3 litres/2¼ pints strong Beef Stock (see page 11)

225 g/8 oz extra lean fresh beef mince

2 tomatoes, peeled, deseeded and chopped

2 large carrots, chopped

1 large onion, chopped

2 celery sticks, chopped

1 turnip, chopped (optional)

1 bouquet garni

2 egg whites

shells of 2 eggs, crushed

salt and pepper

1–2 tbsp sherry (optional)

Melba toast, to serve (optional)

TO GARNISH

julienne strips of raw carrot, turnip, celery or celeriac

NUTRITIONAL INFORMATION

Calories 109

Protein 13g

Carbohydrate 7g

Sugars 6g

Fat 3g

Saturates 1g

variation

For the garnish, replace the julienne strips of raw vegetables with a one-egg omelette, cut into thin strips.

cook's tip

You will find it much easier to whisk the consommé hard when it has reached to almost boiling point if you use a balloon whisk.

1 Place the Beef Stock and beef mince in a large, heavy-based saucepan and leave to stand for 1 hour. Add the tomatoes, carrots, onion, celery, turnip, if using, bouquet garni, egg whites, the crushed shells of 2 eggs and plenty of salt and pepper and bring to almost boiling point, whisking hard all the time with a whisk.

2 Cover and simmer for 1 hour, taking care not to allow the layer of froth on top of the soup to break.

3 Pour the soup through a jelly bag or scalded fine cloth, keeping the froth back until the last, then pour the ingredients through the cloth again into a clean saucepan. The resulting liquid should be clear. Add the sherry, if using, to the soup and reheat gently until hot. Place the garnish in 4 warmed soup bowls and carefully ladle the soup on top. Serve immediately with Melba toast, if you like.

carrot, apple & celery soup

cook: 40 mins   prep: 30 mins   serves 4

NUTRITIONAL INFORMATION

Calories 153

Protein 2g

Carbohydrate 36g

Sugars 34g

Fat 1g

Saturates 0.2g

variation

Substitute 1 large potato, peeled and chopped instead of the celery and garnish with a few sprigs of fresh parsley, if you like.

For this delicious fresh-tasting soup, use your favourite variety of eating apple rather than a cooking variety, which will give too tart a flavour. This soup is the perfect choice for the start of a special-occasion meal or as part of a light lunch.

INGREDIENTS

900 g/2 lb carrots, finely diced

1 medium onion, chopped

3 celery sticks, diced

1 litre/1¾ pints Vegetable Stock (see page 11)

3 medium-sized eating apples

2 tbsp tomato purée

1 bay leaf

2 tsp caster sugar

¼ large lemon

salt and pepper

celery leaves, shredded, to garnish

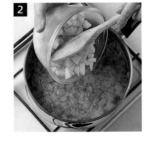

cook's tip

To core whole apples easily, push an apple corer into the stalk end of the apple and twist to cut around the core, then gently pull it out.

1 Place the carrots, onion and celery in a large saucepan and add the Vegetable Stock. Bring to the boil, reduce the heat, cover and simmer for 10 minutes.

2 Meanwhile, peel, core and dice 2 of the apples. Add the diced apple, tomato purée, bay leaf and sugar to the saucepan and

bring to the boil over a medium heat. Reduce the heat, partially cover and simmer for 20 minutes. Remove and discard the bay leaf.

3 Meanwhile, wash, core and cut the remaining apple into thin slices, without peeling. Place the apple slices in a small saucepan and squeeze over the lemon juice.

Heat the apple slices gently and simmer for 1–2 minutes, or until the apple is tender.

4 Drain the apple slices and reserve until required. Place the carrot and apple mixture in a blender or food processor and process until smooth. Alternatively, press the mixture through a sieve with the back of a

wooden spoon. Gently reheat the soup if necessary and season to taste with salt and pepper. Ladle the soup into 4 warmed bowls, top with the reserved apple slices and shredded celery leaves and serve immediately.

chinese noodle soup

This soup has everything going for it – not only is it extremely low in fat, but it takes little time to make, looks intriguing and is a mouthwatering combination of flavours and textures.

INGREDIENTS

1.2 litres/2 pints Vegetable Stock
(see page 11)

2 tbsp light soy sauce

1½ tsp saffron threads

4 spring onions

2 courgettes

2 large tomatoes

1 garlic clove

115 g/4 oz rice noodles

pepper

finely snipped fresh garlic chives,
to garnish

NUTRITIONAL INFORMATION

Calories	135
Protein	. . . . .3g
Carbohydrate	. . . . .29g
Sugars	. . . . .3g
Fat	. . . . .1g
Saturates	. . . . .0g

variation

To give the soup a spicy lift, season with 1–2 pinches of cayenne pepper instead of the ground black pepper.

1 Pour the Vegetable Stock into a large, heavy-based saucepan, add the light soy sauce, then bring the mixture to the boil over a medium heat.

2 Place the saffron threads into a mortar and lightly crush with a pestle, then stir the crushed saffron threads into the hot stock.

3 Prepare the vegetables. Slice the spring onions into rings, then cut the courgettes into batons and peel and chop the tomatoes. Chop the garlic finely, then add all the vegetables to the stock with the rice noodles. Return the soup to the boil over a medium heat, then cover and simmer for 5 minutes.

4 Season the soup to taste with pepper and ladle into 4 warmed serving bowls. Garnish with finely snipped garlic chives and serve immediately.

spicy vegetable soup

⏱ **cook: 15 mins**   ⏱ **prep: 5 mins**   **serves 4**

Wake up the taste buds with a hint of curry spices in this easy-to-prepare vegetable soup. Served as a light lunch with Indian bread, such as chapati or paratha, it is a healthy option.

NUTRITIONAL INFORMATION	
Calories	.75
Protein	.3g
Carbohydrate	.8g
Sugars	.5g
Fat	.4g
Saturates	.1g

INGREDIENTS

1 tbsp sunflower or corn oil

280 g/10 oz leeks, thinly sliced

2 garlic cloves, finely chopped

½ tsp grated fresh root ginger

½ tsp ground cumin

½ tsp ground coriander

½ tsp ground turmeric

1.2 litres/2 pints Vegetable Stock
(see page 11)

450 g/1 lb tomatoes, finely diced

2 courgettes, cut into batons

salt and pepper

3 tbsp chopped fresh coriander, to garnish

variation

For a more subtle flavour to this soup, substitute ½ teaspoon crushed saffron threads for the ground turmeric.

1 Heat the oil in a large, heavy-based saucepan. Add the sliced leeks, chopped garlic and ginger and cook over a medium heat, stirring occasionally, for 2 minutes. Stir in the cumin, ground coriander and turmeric and cook, stirring constantly, for 30 seconds.

2 Pour in the Vegetable Stock and stir well, then bring the mixture to the boil. Reduce the heat, cover and simmer for 5 minutes, then stir in the diced tomatoes and courgette batons. Cover and simmer for a further 3 minutes.

3 Season the soup to taste with salt and pepper, then ladle into 4 warmed serving bowls. Garnish with the chopped fresh coriander and serve.

easy gazpacho

serves 4

prep: 10 mins,
plus 2 hrs chilling

cook: 0 mins

The perfect choice for al fresco dining, this classic chilled soup is packed with fresh flavours. As no cooking is involved, the vegetables retain their colour and their valuable vitamins, and you remain cool in the kitchen.

INGREDIENTS

1 small cucumber, peeled and chopped

2 red peppers, deseeded and chopped

2 green peppers, deseeded and chopped

2 garlic cloves, roughly chopped

1 fresh basil sprig

600 ml/1 pint passata

1 tbsp extra virgin olive oil

1 tbsp red wine vinegar

1 tbsp balsamic vinegar

300 ml/10 fl oz Vegetable Stock

(see page 11)

2 tbsp lemon juice

salt and pepper

TO SERVE

2 tbsp diced, peeled cucumber

2 tbsp finely chopped red onion

2 tbsp finely chopped red pepper

2 tbsp finely chopped green pepper

ice cubes

4 fresh basil sprigs

fresh crusty bread

NUTRITIONAL INFORMATION

Calories	.85
Protein	.3g
Carbohydrate	.11g
Sugars	.10g
Fat	.3g
Saturates	.1g

variation

For a spicier version, add 1 roughly chopped onion with the cucumber in Step 1 and add 1–2 deseeded, finely chopped fresh chillies to the garnishes.

cook's tip

This is a perfect soup to have on a summer picnic. Add the ice cubes to the soup before transferring it to a large flask.

1 Place the cucumber, peppers, garlic and basil in a food processor and process for 1½ minutes. Add the passata, olive oil and both kinds of vinegar and process again until smooth.

2 Pour in the Vegetable Stock and lemon juice and stir. Transfer the mixture to a large bowl. Season to taste with salt and pepper. Cover with clingfilm and leave to chill in the refrigerator for at least 2 hours.

3 To serve, prepare the cucumber, onion and peppers, then place in small serving dishes or arrange decoratively on a plate. Place ice cubes in 4 large soup bowls. Stir the soup and ladle it into the bowls. Garnish with the basil sprigs and serve with the prepared vegetables and chunks of fresh crusty bread.

parisian pea soup

serves 4 **prep: 10 mins** ⌛ **cook: 15–20 mins** ⏱

This is one occasion when cooking with just a little amount of butter is worthwhile because of its rather rich flavour.

INGREDIENTS

25 g/1 oz butter

2 shallots, finely chopped

450 g/1 lb shelled peas

2 Little Gem or 1 small cos or Webbs lettuce, shredded

1.2 litres/2 pints Vegetable Stock (see page 11)

pinch of freshly grated nutmeg

salt and pepper

2–3 tbsp low-fat soured cream (optional)

fresh chives, to garnish

NUTRITIONAL INFORMATION

Calories	.148
Protein	.8g
Carbohydrate	.14g
Sugars	.4g
Fat	.7g
Saturates	.4g

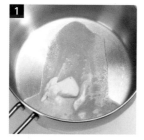

cook's tip

Using home-made Chicken Stock (see page 11) instead of the Vegetable Stock gives this delicate soup a fuller flavour, but also increases the amount of fat slightly.

1 Melt the butter in a large, heavy-based saucepan. Add the shallots and cook over a medium heat, stirring occasionally, for 5 minutes, or until softened.

2 Add the peas, shredded lettuce and Vegetable Stock to the saucepan and season to taste with nutmeg, salt and pepper. Bring to the boil, then reduce the heat, cover and simmer for 10–15 minutes, or until the peas are tender.

3 Remove the saucepan from the heat and leave to cool slightly. Transfer the mixture to a blender or food processor and process until a smooth purée forms. Return the soup to the rinsed-out saucepan and heat through gently until hot. Ladle the soup into 4 large, warmed serving bowls. Top with a spoonful of soured cream, if using, garnish with a few fresh chives and serve.

lentil & tomato soup

⏲ **cook: 50 mins**   ⏱ **prep: 20 mins**   **serves 4**

*This fresh-tasting and colourful soup is substantial enough to serve
on its own with some crusty fresh bread for a light lunch or supper.*

NUTRITIONAL INFORMATION	
Calories	.158
Protein	.9g
Carbohydrate	.24g
Sugars	. 6g
Fat	.4g
Saturates	.1g

INGREDIENTS

1 tbsp corn or sunflower oil

1 onion, finely chopped

1 garlic glove, crushed

½ tsp ground cumin

½ tsp ground coriander

450 g/1 lb tomatoes, peeled, deseeded
and chopped

125 g/4½ oz split red lentils

1.2 litres/2 pints Vegetable Stock
(see page 11)

salt and pepper

finely chopped fresh coriander,
to garnish

cook's tip

Always season lentils with
salt after they have been
cooked, otherwise they will
become tough and may
spoil the finished dish.

1 Heat the oil in a large
saucepan. Add the
onion and cook over a low
heat, stirring occasionally, for
5 minutes, or until softened.

2 Stir in the garlic, cumin,
ground coriander,
tomatoes and lentils and cook,
stirring constantly, for a further
4 minutes. Pour in the stock,
bring to the boil, then reduce

the heat and simmer gently for
30–40 minutes, or until the
lentils are tender. Season to
taste with salt and pepper.

3 Remove the saucepan
from the heat and leave
to cool slightly, then transfer
the mixture to a blender or
food processor and process
until a smooth purée forms.
Return the soup to the

rinsed-out saucepan and
reheat gently until hot.
Ladle the soup into 4 large,
warmed soup bowls, garnish
with chopped fresh coriander
and serve immediately.

mushroom & ginger soup

cook: 15 mins

**prep: 10 mins, plus
30 mins soaking (optional)**

serves 4

*Thai soups are very quickly and easily put together, and
are cooked so that each ingredient can still be tasted in
the finished dish.*

INGREDIENTS

15 g/½ oz dried Chinese mushrooms

1 litre/1¾ pints hot Vegetable Stock
(see page 11)

125 g/4½ oz thread egg noodles

2 tsp sunflower oil

3 garlic cloves, crushed

2.5-cm/1-inch piece fresh root ginger,
finely shredded

½ tsp mushroom ketchup

1 tsp light soy sauce

125 g/4½ oz beansprouts

fresh coriander sprigs, to garnish

variation

Replace the dried Chinese mushrooms
with 125 g/4½ oz fresh field or
chestnut mushrooms, sliced, if
you prefer.

cook's tip

Rice noodles are already
cooked so only need
minimum cooking. They
contain no fat and are ideal
for anyone on a low-fat diet.

1 Soak the dried Chinese
mushrooms, if using,
for at least 30 minutes in
300 ml/10 fl oz of the hot
Vegetable Stock. Remove
the stalks and discard, then
slice the mushrooms. Reserve
the stock. Cook the noodles in
boiling water for 2–3 minutes,
then drain and rinse. Reserve
until required.

2 Heat the sunflower oil
in a preheated wok or
large, heavy-based frying pan
over a high heat. Add the
garlic and ginger, stir and add
the mushrooms. Stir over a
high heat for 2 minutes.

3 Add the remaining
Vegetable Stock
with the reserved stock and
bring to the boil. Add the
mushroom ketchup and soy
sauce. Stir in the beansprouts
and cook until tender. Place
some cooked noodles into
each soup bowl and ladle the
soup on top. Garnish with a
few fresh coriander sprigs and
serve immediately.

fragrant chicken soup

serves 4 **prep: 10 mins** **cook: 15 mins**

This fiery soup is very popular in Thailand, where it is often sold from roadside stalls as a snack. If you prefer a milder flavour, reduce the number of chillies or choose a milder variety.

INGREDIENTS

2 lemon grass stalks

400 ml/14 fl oz coconut milk

3 kaffir lime leaves, torn into small pieces

5-cm/2-inch piece galangal or fresh root ginger, sliced

700 ml/1¼ pints water

500 g/1 lb 2 oz skinless, boneless chicken breasts, trimmed of all visible fat and cut into thin strips

225 g/8 oz shiitake mushrooms, chopped

2 tomatoes, cut into wedges

3 fresh bird's eye chillies, deseeded and thinly sliced

3 tbsp lime juice

2 tbsp Thai fish sauce (nam pla)

fresh coriander leaves, to garnish

NUTRITIONAL INFORMATION	
Calories	190
Protein	30g
Carbohydrate	8g
Sugars	7g
Fat	5g
Saturates	2g

variation

You could also make this soup with peeled, raw tiger prawns or, for a vegetarian alternative, use cubes of firm tofu instead of the chicken strips.

cook's tip

Be careful when handling fresh chillies, as they can burn. Wearing rubber gloves is a wise precaution and you should always wash your hands thoroughly afterwards.

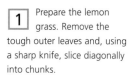

1 Prepare the lemon grass. Remove the tough outer leaves and, using a sharp knife, slice diagonally into chunks.

2 Pour the coconut milk into a large, heavy-based saucepan, add the lemon grass, kaffir lime leaves and galangal. Bring to the boil, then reduce the heat and simmer for 2 minutes. Add the water and return to the boil. Add the chicken strips, mushrooms and tomatoes and simmer for 5 minutes, or until the chicken strips are tender.

3 Stir in the chillies, lime juice and Thai fish sauce. Using a slotted spoon, remove and discard the lemon grass and galangal. Ladle the soup into 4 large, warmed soup bowls, garnish with a few fresh coriander leaves and serve immediately.

cock-a-leekie soup

cook: 2 hrs   **prep: 30 mins**   **serves 4–6**

NUTRITIONAL INFORMATION	
Calories	.45
Protein	.5g
Carbohydrate	5g
Sugars	.4g
Fat	.1g
Saturates	0.2g

variation

You can replace the Chicken Stock with 3 chicken stock cubes dissolved in the same amount of water, if you prefer.

A traditional Scottish soup in which a whole chicken is cooked with the vegetables to add extra flavour to the stock. In some areas, the soup was eaten as a first course, then the cooked chicken was served as part of the main course.

INGREDIENTS

1–1.5 kg/2 lb 4 oz–3 lb 5 oz oven-ready chicken, plus giblets, if available

1.75–2 litres/3–3½ pints Chicken Stock (see page 11)

1 onion, sliced

4 leeks, thinly sliced

pinch of ground allspice or ground coriander

1 bouquet garni

salt and pepper

12 ready-to-eat prunes, halved and stoned

warm crusty bread, to serve

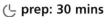

cook's tip

If ready-to-eat prunes are not available, then use dried prunes instead. Put 12 dried prunes in a bowl and pour over enough water to cover. Leave to soak overnight.

1 Place the chicken, giblets, if using, Chicken Stock and onion in a large, heavy-based saucepan. Bring to the boil and skim off any scum that rises to the surface with a slotted spoon.

2 Add the leeks, ground allspice or coriander and the bouquet garni to the saucepan, season to taste with salt and pepper, cover and simmer gently for 1½ hours, or until the chicken flesh is falling off the bones. Remove the chicken and bouquet garni from the saucepan and skim off any fat from the surface of the soup.

3 Chop some of the chicken flesh and return to the saucepan. Add the prunes, return to the boil and simmer, uncovered, for 20 minutes. Taste and adjust the seasoning, if necessary. Ladle into a large, warmed soup tureen and serve immediately with warm crusty bread.

rosy melon & strawberries

serves 4　　**prep: 10 mins, plus 2 hrs** ⏲　　**cook: 0 mins** ⏲
15 mins chilling/standing

The delicate combination of sweet melon and fresh strawberries macerated in rosé wine and a hint of rosewater is a delightful start to a special meal. Always wash rose petals thoroughly and check that they are free from any blemishes and pesticides.

INGREDIENTS

¼ **honeydew melon**

½ **Charentais melon**

150 ml/5 fl oz **rosé wine**

2–3 tsp **rosewater**

175 g/6 oz **small strawberries,
washed and hulled**

rose petals, to garnish

NUTRITIONAL INFORMATION	
Calories 59	
Protein 1g	
Carbohydrate 8g	
Sugars 8g	
Fat 0g	
Saturates 20g	

variation

Other varieties of melon can also be used in this recipe. Try Galia and Cantaloupe instead.

cook's tip

Rosewater for culinary use is generally available from large pharmacies and leading supermarkets as well as from more specialist food suppliers.

1 Scoop out the seeds from both melons with a spoon. Using a sharp knife, carefully remove the skin, taking care not to remove too much flesh.

2 Cut the melon flesh into thin strips and place in a large bowl. Pour over the wine and enough rosewater to taste. Mix together gently, cover with clingfilm and leave to chill in the refrigerator for at least 2 hours.

3 Halve the strawberries and carefully mix into the melon. Leave the melon and strawberries to stand at room temperature for 15 minutes to let the flavours develop – if the melon is too cold, there will be little flavour. Arrange on 4 large serving plates and garnish with a few rose petals. Serve immediately.

prawn-filled artichokes

serves 4

prep: 15 mins, plus 10 mins cooling

cook: 40–50 mins

Globe artichokes filled with a delicious stir-fried mix of prawns, garlic, tomatoes and spring onions make an attractive and adventurous starter for a dinner party.

INGREDIENTS

6 tbsp lemon juice

4 globe artichokes

1 tbsp olive or sunflower oil

6 spring onions, finely chopped

1 garlic clove, finely chopped

350 g/12 oz raw prawns, peeled

6 tomatoes, peeled, deseeded and diced

grated rind of 1 lemon

salt and pepper

grated lemon zest, to garnish

NUTRITIONAL INFORMATION	
Calories	172
Protein	25g
Carbohydrate	9g
Sugars	7g
Fat	5g
Saturates	1g

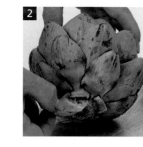

variation

If raw prawns are not available, use cooked ones instead. Heat them just long enough to warm them through.

1 Fill a large bowl with cold water and add 2 tablespoons of lemon juice.

2 Working on one artichoke at a time, twist off the stalks, cut the bases flat and pull off any small, tough base leaves. Slice off the tops and trim the tips of the leaves with kitchen scissors. Place in the acidulated water.

3 Bring a large saucepan of water to the boil, add the remaining lemon juice and the artichokes, cover and cook for 30–40 minutes, or until a leaf comes away easily from the bases. Remove from the pan and invert to drain. Leave to cool.

4 Heat the olive oil in a large frying pan or preheated wok over a medium–high heat. Add the finely chopped spring onions and garlic and stir-fry for 3–4 minutes, then add the prawns and stir-fry for a further 3 minutes, or until they change colour. Stir in the diced tomatoes and lemon rind and season to taste with salt and pepper. Remove the frying pan from the heat.

5 When the artichokes are cool enough to handle, remove and discard the chokes. Spoon the stir-fried prawns into the centre of the artichokes and garnish with grated lemon zest. Serve warm.

antipasto mushrooms

cook: 30 mins

**prep: 10 mins,
plus 30 mins cooling**

serves 4

*Traditionally, porcini mushrooms, also known as ceps, would be
used for this dish, but you can make it with any of your favourite
varieties, such as oyster, chanterelles and even button mushrooms.*

NUTRITIONAL INFORMATION	
Calories	100
Protein	3g
Carbohydrate	2g
Sugars	2g
Fat	9g
Saturates	1g

INGREDIENTS

3 tbsp olive oil

2 garlic cloves, finely chopped

225 g/8 oz tomatoes, peeled,
deseeded and finely chopped

1 tbsp finely chopped fresh oregano

salt and pepper

500 g/1 lb 2 oz open-cap and closed-
cup mushrooms

fresh flat-leaved parsley sprigs,
to garnish

crusty bread, to serve

cook's tip

If you want to use dried
porcini mushrooms, soak
15 g/½ oz mushrooms in
boiling water for 20 minutes,
or until soft. Drain, then add
to the rest of the mushrooms
in the frying pan in Step 2.

1 Heat 1 tablespoon of
the olive oil in a large,
heavy-based saucepan, add
the garlic and cook over a low
heat, stirring constantly, for
1 minute. Add the tomatoes
and oregano and season to
taste with salt and pepper.
Cook over a low heat, stirring
frequently, for 20 minutes,
or until the mixture is pulpy
and thickened.

2 Using a sharp knife,
slice the mushrooms
thinly. Heat the remaining olive
oil in a large frying pan. Add
the mushrooms and cook over
a medium heat, stirring
frequently, for 5 minutes, or
until tender. Stir the mushrooms
into the tomato mixture and
season with salt. Reduce the
heat, cover and simmer for a
further 10 minutes.

3 Transfer the mushroom
mixture to a bowl and
leave to cool. Transfer to a
large serving dish, garnish with
flat-leaved parsley and serve
at room temperature with
crusty bread.

mexican vegetable platter

serves 4 **prep: 10 mins,** ↻ **plus 40 mins chilling** **cook: 8 mins** ⟳

Known as pico de gallo, *this tempting selection of chilled vegetables and fruit is served with a spicy red pepper and chilli purée. It makes a refreshing starter to a summer supper.*

INGREDIENTS

2 tsp sunflower or corn oil

1 red pepper, deseeded and diced

juice of 1 small orange

juice of 1 lime

1–2 fresh red chillies, deseeded and finely chopped

200 g/7 oz carrots

1 cucumber

½ pineapple

1 mango

½ bunch of fresh mint

NUTRITIONAL INFORMATION

Calories 96

Protein 2g

Carbohydrate 19g

Sugars 18g

Fat 2g

Saturates 0g

variation

Other vegetables and fruit can be used. Include slices of avocado, brushed with lime juice to prevent discoloration, and chunks of papaya.

cook's tip

Choose firm, slightly underripe mangoes, which slice easily. Using a sharp knife, peel the mango completely, then carefully slice around the stone.

1 First, make the pepper purée. Heat the sunflower oil in a large frying pan and add the pepper. Cook over a medium heat, stirring occasionally for 2 minutes. Add the orange and lime juice and cook for a further 5 minutes. Remove from the heat and leave to cool slightly, then transfer to a blender or food processor and process

until a smooth purée forms. Transfer to a small serving bowl and add the chopped chillies. Cover with clingfilm and chill in the refrigerator until ready to serve.

2 Peel the carrots and cut into thin diagonal slices. Peel the cucumber, cut in half and, using a teaspoon, scoop out the seeds, then thinly slice.

3 Cut the plume off the pineapple and discard. Cut the pineapple into quarters, lengthways. Stand the quarters upright and cut away the central core. Slice off the skin with a sharp knife, remove any eyes and cut into cubes. Peel the mango and slice the flesh. Discard the stone. Arrange the fruit and vegetables decoratively on a

large serving plate. Cover and leave to chill in the refrigerator for 15 minutes.

4 Slice or tear the mint leaves into thin strips. Spoon the pepper purée over the chilled vegetables, sprinkle with the mint and serve.

crudités with garlic chive & coriander dip

serves 4   **prep: 10 mins** ☾   **cook: 2 mins** ☕

Raw vegetables are the ideal healthy start to a meal, but creamy dips can undo all your good intentions. This is the perfect solution – all the richness and flavour, but none of the fat.

INGREDIENTS

CRUDITÉS	DIP
115 g/4 oz baby corn cobs	1 tbsp hot water
115 g/4 oz young asparagus spears, trimmed	1 tsp saffron threads
1 head of chicory, leaves separated	225 g/8 oz fat-free fromage frais
1 red pepper, deseeded and sliced	3 tbsp chopped fresh coriander
1 orange pepper, deseeded and sliced	1 tbsp snipped fresh garlic chives
8 radishes, trimmed	salt and pepper
	fresh coriander sprigs, to garnish

NUTRITIONAL INFORMATION

Calories	.67
Protein	.7g
Carbohydrate	.9g
Sugars	.8g
Fat	.1g
Saturates	.0g

variation

Try using different selections of vegetables, such as celery sticks, trimmed spring onions, strips of cucumber and carrot batons.

cook's tip

The fat content of fromage frais ranges between 0 and 8 per cent. This is reflected in the consistency. Fat-free fromage frais is great for dips because it is soft and easily mixed with other ingredients.

1 Blanch the corn and asparagus in separate saucepans of boiling water for 2 minutes. Drain, plunge into iced water and drain again. Arrange all the vegetables on a serving platter and cover with a damp tea towel.

2 For the dip, place the water in a small bowl. Lightly crush the saffron threads between your fingers and add to the bowl, then leave to stand for 3–4 minutes, or until the water is a rich golden colour.

3 Place the fromage frais into a separate bowl and beat until smooth, then beat in the infused saffron water. Stir in the chopped coriander and snipped chives and season to taste with salt and pepper. Transfer to a serving bowl and garnish with a few sprigs of fresh coriander. Serve immediately with the prepared vegetables.

bruschetta

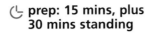

cook: 5 mins

prep: 15 mins, plus 30 mins standing

serves 4

NUTRITIONAL INFORMATION

Calories	161
Protein	1g
Carbohydrate	20g
Sugars	161g
Fat	1g
Saturates	20g

Traditionally, this Italian savoury is enriched with olive oil. Here, sundried tomatoes are a good substitute and only a little oil is used.

INGREDIENTS

60 g/2¼ oz dry-pack sun-dried tomatoes

300 ml/10 fl oz boiling water

35-cm/14-inch long Granary or wholemeal stick of French bread

1 large garlic clove, halved

25 g/1 oz stoned black olives in brine, drained and quartered

2 tsp olive oil

salt and pepper

2 tbsp chopped fresh basil

40 g/1½ oz grated low-fat mozzarella cheese

TO GARNISH

shredded fresh basil leaves

fresh basil sprigs

variation

Make your own topping, such as cherry tomatoes, capers, a few shavings of fresh Parmesan cheese and fresh tarragon leaves to garnish.

cook's tip

If you use sun-dried tomatoes packed in oil, drain them, rinse in warm water and drain again on kitchen paper. Though less rich in flavour, thinly sliced fresh tomatoes can be used instead.

1 Place the sun-dried tomatoes in a small heatproof bowl and pour over the boiling water. Leave to stand for 30 minutes to soften. Drain well and pat dry with kitchen paper. Slice into thin strips and reserve.

2 Preheat the grill to medium. Trim and discard the ends of the bread and cut into 12 slices. Arrange on a grill rack and cook under the preheated hot grill for 1–2 minutes on each side until golden. Rub both sides of each piece of bread with the cut sides of the garlic. Top with strips of sun-dried tomato and olives.

3 Brush lightly with olive oil and season well with salt and pepper. Sprinkle with the chopped fresh basil and grated mozzarella cheese and return to the grill for 1–2 minutes, or until the cheese is melted and bubbling. Transfer to a warmed serving platter and garnish with shredded basil leaves and sprigs of basil. Serve immediately.

parsley, chicken & ham pâté

serves 4

prep: 25 mins,
plus 30 mins chilling

cook: 0 mins

Pâté is easy to make at home, and this combination of lean chicken and ham mixed with herbs is especially straightforward.

INGREDIENTS

225 g/8 oz skinless, boneless, lean
chicken, cooked

100 g/3½ oz lean ham

small bunch of fresh parsley

1 garlic clove, peeled

1 tsp grated lime rind

2 tbsp lime juice

125 ml/4 fl oz low-fat fromage frais

salt and pepper

lime zest, to garnish

TO SERVE

lime wedges

crispbread or Melba toast

NUTRITIONAL INFORMATION	
Calories 119	
Protein 20g	
Carbohydrate 2g	
Sugars 2g	
Fat 3g	
Saturates 1g	

variation

This pâté can also be
made with minced, lean,
cooked turkey, beef or
pork, or with prawns,
white crabmeat or tuna.

1 Finely chop the chicken, ham, parsley and garlic and place in a large bowl, then mix together.

2 Add the lime rind and juice and mix well. Alternatively, finely chop the chicken and ham and place in a blender or food processor. Finely chop the parsley and garlic and add to the blender or food processor with the lime rind and juice and process until finely minced. Transfer the mixture to a large bowl.

3 Using a metal spoon, mix in the fromage frais, then season to taste with salt and pepper, cover with clingfilm and leave to chill in the refrigerator for 30 minutes.

4 Pile the pâté into individual serving dishes and garnish with lime zest. Serve the pâtés with lime wedges and crispbread.

spinach cheese moulds

⏲ **cook: 50 mins**　　　⏱ **prep: 50 mins,
plus 1 hr chilling**　　　**serves 4**

These flavour-packed little moulds are a perfect starter for a special-occasion meal or a light lunch. Serve with warmed pitta bread.

NUTRITIONAL INFORMATION	
Calories	.119
Protein	.6g
Carbohydrates	.2g
Sugars	.2g
Fat	.9g
Saturates	.6g

INGREDIENTS

100 g/3½ oz fresh spinach leaves

300 g/10½ oz skimmed milk soft cheese

2 garlic cloves, crushed

few sprigs of fresh parsley,
finely chopped

salt and pepper

TO SERVE

salad leaves and fresh herbs

warmed pitta bread

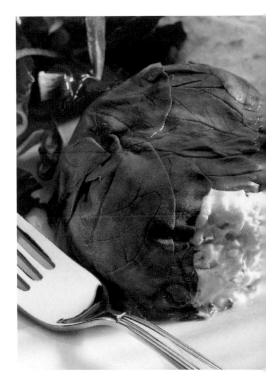

variation

Replace the chopped fresh parsley with fresh tarragon or chives. A mix of all of these herbs would work equally well.

1 Trim the stalks from the spinach leaves and discard, then rinse the leaves thoroughly under cold running water. Pack the wet leaves into a small saucepan, cover and cook for 3–4 minutes, or until wilted. Drain and pat dry with kitchen paper. Line the bases of 4 small pudding basins or individual ramekin dishes with baking paper, then line the basins or ramekin dishes with the wilted spinach leaves so that the leaves overhang the edges of the basins.

2 Place the cheese in a small bowl and add the crushed garlic and chopped fresh parsley. Mix together thoroughly until blended, then season to taste with salt and pepper.

3 Spoon the cheese and herb mixture into the prepared basins or ramekin dishes and cover the cheese with the overhanging spinach. Alternatively, lay extra leaves to cover the top. Place a greaseproof paper circle on top of each dish and weigh down with a 100 g/3½ oz weight. Leave to chill in the refrigerator for 1 hour.

4 Remove the weights and peel off the paper. Loosen the moulds gently by running a small palette knife around the edges of each dish and turn them out on to 4 serving plates. Serve the moulds with a mixture of salad leaves and fresh herbs, and warmed pitta bread.

chicken & asparagus timbales

serves 4

prep: 15–20 mins, ⟳
plus 1 hr 10 mins chilling

cook: 30 mins ⟳

These elegant little moulds would make a wonderful starter for a dinner party. They are packed with flavour, yet light and melt-in-the-mouth, and they look quite stunning. Although they take some time and effort to prepare, the results are worth it.

INGREDIENTS

1 lemon	115 g/4 oz young asparagus
2 skinless, boneless chicken	spears, trimmed
breasts, about 115 g/4 oz each,	2 tbsp white wine
trimmed of all visible fat	1 sachet powdered gelatine
2 fresh tarragon sprigs	100 g/3½ oz fat-free fromage frais
150 ml/5 fl oz water	1 tsp chopped fresh tarragon
salt and pepper	

NUTRITIONAL INFORMATION

Calories 92
Protein 15g
Carbohydrate 2g
Sugars 2g
Fat 2g
Saturates 1g

variation

Substitute fresh rosemary or thyme instead of tarragon, but use them sparingly as they have an intense flavour and may overwhelm the dish.

cook's tip

When heating gelatine over a saucepan of simmering water, make sure the gelatine does not boil as it will become stringy and will spoil the finished dish.

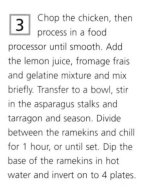

1 Cut a strip of rind from the lemon. Squeeze the juice and reserve. Place the lemon rind, chicken, tarragon sprigs and water in a saucepan and season to taste. Cover, bring to the boil, then reduce the heat to low and cook for 20 minutes, or until the meat is tender. Remove the chicken with a slotted spoon and cool. Sieve and reserve the cooking liquid. Blanch the asparagus for 5 minutes. Drain, then cut off and reserve 4 cm/1½ inches of the tips. Chop the stalks.

2 Place the reserved cooking liquid in a jug. Make up to 150 ml/5 fl oz with water, if necessary. Stir in the wine. Place 4 tablespoons of the mixture in a heatproof bowl, sprinkle ½ teaspoon of gelatine on top, leave for 2 minutes, then set over a saucepan of simmering water. Stir for 2–3 minutes. Divide between 4 ramekins and chill for 5 minutes. Arrange 2 asparagus tips, facing in opposite directions, in each ramekin and chill until set. Dissolve the remaining gelatine in the remaining stock and wine, as before.

3 Chop the chicken, then process in a food processor until smooth. Add the lemon juice, fromage frais and gelatine mixture and mix briefly. Transfer to a bowl, stir in the asparagus stalks and tarragon and season. Divide between the ramekins and chill for 1 hour, or until set. Dip the base of the ramekins in hot water and invert on to 4 plates.

chinese pot stickers

serves 6 **prep: 30 mins** **cook: 50–60 mins**

These tasty chicken- and vegetable-filled dumplings are equally suitable for serving as part of a Chinese meal or as a starter before a Western main course. You can also serve them with plain dark soy sauce or chilli sauce for dipping, if you like.

INGREDIENTS

175 g/6 oz Chinese leaves, shredded

1 litre/1¾ pints boiling water

115 g/4 oz lean chicken mince

5 canned water chestnuts, drained, rinsed and chopped

1 spring onion, finely chopped

1 tablespoon Chinese rice wine

1 teaspoon light soy sauce

1 tsp cornflour

pepper

24 wonton wrappers, thawed if frozen

groundnut or sunflower oil, for brushing

DIPPING SAUCE

125 ml/4 fl oz Vegetable Stock (see page 11)

1 tbsp caster sugar

3 tbsp dark soy sauce

shredded fresh coriander

NUTRITIONAL INFORMATION

Calories 109

Protein 7g

Carbohydrate 19g

Sugars 4g

Fat 1g

Saturates 0g

variation

You can substitute the same quantity of lean minced steak or chopped peeled raw prawns for the chicken, if you like.

cook's tip

Cook the pot stickers in batches, as they should not touch each other during the process. When steaming, add enough water to come about halfway up the sides of the pot stickers.

1 First, make the dipping sauce by mixing all the ingredients in a small bowl, stirring until the sugar has dissolved, then reserve.

2 Place the Chinese leaves in a colander and pour over the boiling water. Drain well, pressing the leaves with the back of a spoon. Transfer the Chinese leaves to a large

bowl with the chicken, water chestnuts, spring onion, Chinese rice wine, soy sauce and cornflour. Season to taste with pepper and mix well. Spread out 1 wonton wrapper and place a teaspoon of the filling in the centre. Brush the edge with water and fold to make a half moon. Press the edges together to seal and crimp the rim slightly. Gently

curve the dumpling by pinching the ends of the rim between your forefingers and thumbs. Make the remaining dumplings in the same way.

3 Brush the base of a non-stick wok or frying pan with groundnut oil and set over a medium heat. Add 5–6 dumplings in a single layer, smooth sides

downwards. Cook for 2–3 minutes, or until golden brown underneath. Add 3–4 tablespoons water, partially cover and steam for 10 minutes, or until cooked through and most of the water has evaporated. Transfer to a serving plate and keep warm. Cook the remaining dumplings, in batches, in the same way. Serve with the dipping sauce.

asparagus with orange dressing

serves 4　　　　**prep: 10 mins,** ⟳　　　　**cook: 10 mins** ⟳
plus 15 mins standing

Asparagus is in season for only a short time and is a special treat in late spring and early summer. Imported asparagus is available all year round, but it may be very expensive.

INGREDIENTS

2 oranges

350 g/12 oz asparagus, trimmed

1 tablespoon lemon juice

1 spring onion, finely chopped

1 garlic clove, finely chopped

2 tbsp extra virgin olive oil

1 tbsp white wine vinegar

NUTRITIONAL INFORMATION	
Calories	.88
Protein	.3g
Carbohydrate	.6g
Sugars	.6g
Fat	.6g
Saturates	.1g

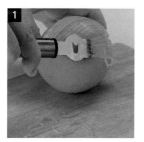

cook's tip

A special asparagus kettle is designed so that the stems cook in the water while the tips are steamed. If you don't have one, use a deep saucepan, tie the asparagus loosely and wedge upright.

1 Bring a small saucepan of water to the boil over a medium heat. Using a zester, cut the rind of both oranges into very thin strips. Reserve the oranges. Add the rind to the saucepan, return the mixture to the boil and simmer for 1 minute. Drain the rind, refresh under cold running water and drain again, then reserve.

2 Bring a large saucepan of water to the boil over a medium heat. Add the asparagus and cook for 5 minutes, or until just tender. Drain the asparagus, refresh under cold running water and drain again. Pat dry with kitchen paper. Arrange the asparagus on a serving dish, cover and chill in the refrigerator until required.

3 To make the orange dressing, squeeze the reserved oranges to make 5 tablespoons of orange juice. Mix the orange juice, lemon juice, spring onion, garlic and orange rind together in a small bowl, then leave to stand at room temperature for 15 minutes to allow the flavours to mingle. Using a balloon whisk, whisk in the

olive oil and vinegar. Pour the dressing over the asparagus and serve immediately.

parma ham with figs

⏲ **cook: 0 mins**   ⏱ **prep: 10 mins, plus 20 mins chilling**   **serves 4**

This classic Italian starter couldn't be easier or more delicious. Parma ham has a uniquely aromatic flavour and is served in paper-thin slices. Succulent fresh figs make a natural partnership.

NUTRITIONAL INFORMATION	
Calories	124
Protein	13g
Carbohydrate	6g
Sugars	5g
Fat	6g
Saturates	2g

INGREDIENTS

175 g/6 oz Parma ham, thinly sliced

pepper

4 fresh figs

1 lime

2 fresh basil sprigs

---

variation

This dish is also delicious made with 4 slices of Charentais melon or 12–16 cooked and cooled asparagus spears, instead of the figs.

---

1 Using a sharp knife, trim the visible fat from the slices of ham and discard. Arrange the ham on 4 large serving plates, loosely folding it so that it falls into decorative shapes. Season to taste with pepper.

2 Using a sharp knife, cut each fig lengthways into 4 wedges. Arrange a fig on each serving plate. Cut the lime into 6 wedges, place a wedge on each plate and reserve the others. Remove the leaves from the basil sprigs and divide between the plates. Cover with clingfilm and leave in the refrigerator to chill until ready to serve.

3 Just before serving, remove the plates from the refrigerator and squeeze the juice from the remaining lime wedges over the ham.

crab cakes with salsa verde

serves 4

prep: 15 mins, ⟳
plus 30–60 mins chilling

cook: 15 mins ⟳

These spicy fish cakes are popular throughout Thailand, where they are eaten as between-meal snacks. Mixing crabmeat with white fish makes the cakes easier to handle and the dish more economical.

INGREDIENTS

250 g/9 oz crabmeat,
thawed if frozen

250 g/9 oz white fish fillet, such as cod,
skinned and roughly chopped

1 fresh red chilli, deseeded and
roughly chopped

1 garlic clove, roughly chopped

2.5-cm/1-inch piece of fresh root
ginger, roughly chopped

1 lemon grass stalk, roughly chopped

3 tbsp chopped fresh coriander

1 egg white

groundnut or sunflower oil, for frying

SALSA VERDE

2 fresh green chillies, deseeded and
roughly chopped

8 spring onions, roughly chopped

2 garlic cloves, roughly chopped

1 bunch of fresh parsley

grated rind and juice of 1 lime

juice of 1 lemon

4 tbsp olive oil

1 tbsp green Tabasco sauce

salt and pepper

NUTRITIONAL INFORMATION

Calories	.318
Protein	.26g
Carbohydrate	.2g
Sugars	.1g
Fat	.23g
Saturates	.3g

variation

For an elegant presentation, garnish the crab cakes with fresh Chinese chives. If these are unavailable, use ordinary fresh chives instead.

cook's tip

Much of the fat in this recipe is contained in the salsa verde dip, so if you would prefer a lower-fat dish, serve only small helpings of the salsa verde. The remainder can be stored in the refrigerator.

1 Place the crabmeat, fish, red chilli, garlic, ginger, lemon grass, coriander and egg white in a food processor and process until thoroughly blended, then transfer to a bowl, cover with clingfilm and chill in the refrigerator for 30–60 minutes.

2 Meanwhile, make the salsa verde. Place the green chillies, spring onions, garlic and parsley in a food processor and process until finely chopped. Transfer to a small bowl and stir in the lime rind, lime and lemon juice, olive oil and green Tabasco sauce. Season to taste with salt and pepper, cover with clingfilm and leave to chill in the refrigerator until ready to serve.

3 Heat 2 tablespoons of the groundnut oil in a non-stick frying pan. Add spoonfuls of the crab mixture, flattening them gently with a spatula and keeping them spaced well apart. Cook for 4 minutes, then turn with a spatula and cook the other side for 3 minutes, or until golden brown. Remove from the frying pan and keep warm while you cook the remaining batches, adding more oil if necessary. Transfer the crab cakes to a large serving plate, garnish and serve with the salsa verde.

trout mousse

serves 6 **prep: 15 mins,** **plus 3 hrs 20 mins chilling** **cook: 15 mins**

This delicate pink mousse makes a superb starter for a dinner party or buffet table. Trout is an oily fish, but contains the 'good' omega-3 essential fatty acids that are vital for wellbeing and protect against heart disease and circulatory problems.

INGREDIENTS

150 ml/5 fl oz Fish Stock (see page 11)

1 tbsp French vermouth

1 tbsp lime juice

1 small onion, finely chopped

250 g/9 oz trout fillets

1 tsp tomato purée

2 tbsp Greek-style yogurt

salt and white pepper

1½ tsp water

½ sachet (1½ tsp) powdered gelatine

1 large egg white

fresh dill sprigs, to garnish

Melba toast (see Cook's Tip) or toasted wholemeal bread, to serve

NUTRITIONAL INFORMATION	
Calories	79
Protein	10g
Carbohydrate	1g
Sugars	1g
Fat	4g
Saturates	1g

variation

This mousse can also be made with sea trout fillets, which also have pink flesh and a delicate flavour.

cook's tip

To make Melba toast, remove the crusts from slices of bread and grill on both sides. Slice through horizontally to give 2 very thin slices. Cut in half diagonally and grill until golden.

1 Pour the Fish Stock into a wide, shallow pan and add the vermouth, lime juice and onion. Bring to the boil, then reduce the heat to low and simmer for 3 minutes. Add the fish fillets, skin-side down, cover and poach for 3 minutes. Remove from the heat and leave, still covered, until cool. Lift out the fish, reserving the stock, then remove and discard the skin and flake the flesh. Sieve the stock into a food processor, add the fish and process until a smooth paste forms. Transfer to a bowl and beat in the tomato purée and yogurt. Season to taste.

2 Pour the water into a small, heatproof bowl and sprinkle the gelatine on the surface. Leave to stand for 2 minutes to soften, then set the bowl over a saucepan of simmering water and stir for 2–3 minutes, or until the gelatine has dissolved. Pour the gelatine mixture into the fish mixture in a steady stream, beating constantly. Chill in the refrigerator for 15–20 minutes, or until just beginning to set.

3 Whisk the egg white until stiff, but not dry. Gently stir one-quarter of the egg white into the fish mixture, then fold in the remainder. Rinse 6 ramekin dishes or bowls with water and spoon in the fish mixture. Smooth the tops, cover and chill in the refrigerator for 2–3 hours, or until set. Garnish with dill sprigs and serve with toast.

artichoke hearts with a warm dressing

serves 4   **prep: 15 mins** ⏲   **cook: 45 mins** ⏱

Artichoke hearts are truly a luxury and taste superb with this warm, nutty dressing. For less fat content, omit the walnut garnish.

INGREDIENTS

250 g/9 oz mixed salad leaves, such as

lollo rosso, escarole and lamb's lettuce

6 tbsp lemon juice

4 globe artichokes

5 tbsp Calvados

1 shallot, very finely chopped

pinch of salt

1 tbsp red wine vinegar

3 tbsp walnut oil

TO GARNISH

55 g/2 oz shelled walnuts, halved

1 tbsp finely chopped fresh parsley

NUTRITIONAL INFORMATION

Calories	.287
Protein	.7g
Carbohydrate	.14g
Sugars	.2g
Fat	.18g
Saturates	.2g

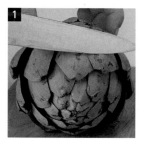

variation

This recipe also works well with good-quality canned or bottled artichoke hearts. Drain and rinse well before using.

1 Place the salad leaves in a bowl and reserve. Fill a bowl with cold water and add 2 tablespoons of the lemon juice. Working on one artichoke at a time, twist off the stalks, cut the bases flat and pull off all the dark outer leaves. Slice the artichokes in half horizontally and discard the top parts. Trim around the bases to remove the outer

dark green layer and place in the acidulated water. Bring a saucepan of water to the boil, add the remaining lemon juice and the artichokes, cover and cook for 30–40 minutes, or until tender. Drain, refresh under cold running water and drain again. Pull off and discard the remaining leaves, slice off and discard the chokes and set the hearts aside.

2 Pour the Calvados into a small saucepan, add the shallot and salt and bring to just below boiling point. Reduce the heat, carefully ignite the Calvados and continue to cook until the flames have died down. Stir in the vinegar and walnut oil and cook, stirring constantly, for 1 minute. Remove the saucepan from the heat.

3 Spoon half the dressing over the salad leaves and toss well to coat. Transfer the salad leaves to a large serving plate and top with the artichoke hearts. Spoon the remaining dressing over the artichoke hearts, garnish with the walnuts and parsley and serve immediately.

oysters rockefeller

cook: 10 mins   **prep: 30 mins**   **serves 6**

This is a variation of the famous New Orleans dish, which is cooked and served on a bed of rock salt. Although an extravagant indulgence, it makes a spectacular starter for a special occasion.

NUTRITIONAL INFORMATION	
Calories	.97
Protein	.13g
Carbohydrate	6g
Sugars	.3g
Fat	.2g
Saturates	.0g

INGREDIENTS

450 g/1 lb fresh spinach leaves

rock salt

36 fresh oysters in their shells

4 spring onions, chopped

2 celery sticks, chopped

3 fresh parsley sprigs

1–2 tbsp low-fat natural yogurt

pinch of cayenne pepper

1 tbsp pastis (see Cook's Tip)

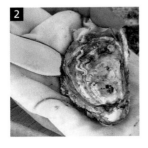

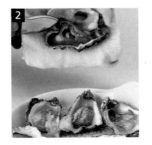

cook's tip

Pastis is an alcoholic drink, which is flavoured with star anise. It is very popular in the south of France. The best-known brand is Pernod.

1 Preheat the oven to 230°C/450°F/Gas Mark 8. Trim the stalks from the spinach leaves and discard, then rinse the leaves under cold running water. Place the leaves into a large saucepan, cover and cook over a medium heat for 3 minutes. Turn the spinach over, cover and cook for a further 2 minutes. Drain well, squeezing out as much liquid as possible, then set aside. Cover the bases of 2 ovenproof dishes with a 1-cm/½-inch layer of rock salt.

2 Wrap a tea towel around one hand and grasp an oyster, flat shell uppermost. Insert a strong knife into the hinge between the shells and twist to prise them open. Run the blade along the inside of the top shell to sever the upper muscle, then along the inside of the lower shell to cut the lower muscle. Discard the top shells. Open the remaining oysters in the same way. Set the shells on the salt layers.

3 Place the spinach, spring onions, celery, parsley, yogurt and cayenne pepper in a food processor and pulse until a smooth purée forms. Transfer to a bowl and stir in the pastis. Cover each oyster with a spoonful of the spinach purée, then bake in the preheated oven for 4 minutes. Serve immediately.

snacks & light meals

There are many occasions when we feel it is time for a 'little something',

but don't want a complete meal. Many popular snacks and easy 'instant' meals – from crisps

and biscuits to pizzas and sausages – are extremely high in fat (as well as salt and sugar),

and it is all too easy to wreck your healthy eating plan. So turn to this chapter, packed with

delicious low-fat snacks and light meals, to solve the problem. There is something for everyone.

Need a quick snack to keep you going in the middle of the day? Try one of the

luscious Scrumptious Sandwiches (see page 62). If the kids come home from school starving and

it's a long way until supper time, make a batch of Falafel (see page 90). Want a light lunch

for guests? How about Cantaloupe & Crab Salad (see page 100)? Need to fuel the family

for an action-packed weekend? Try Mexican Eggs (see page 74). Many of these dishes are also

perfect for school lunch boxes and picnics. Whether you want a hot dish to fill the gap on

a winter's day or to ring the changes with some unusual summer salads,

you are sure to find the perfect healthy choice.

pasta with low-fat pesto

serves 4 **prep: 5 mins** ⟳ **cook: 8–10 mins** ⟳

Pesto is a wonderfully useful sauce that can be served with all kinds of foods, from pasta to baked potatoes, but its great disadvantage is that it contains over 50 g/1¾ oz fat per serving. You can make this sauce without the addition of lots of olive oil, thus reducing its fat content to one-quarter of that of traditional pesto.

INGREDIENTS

225 g/8 oz dried spaghetti or linguine

fresh basil sprigs, to garnish

freshly grated Parmesan cheese, to serve

1 garlic clove, roughly chopped

25 g/1 oz pine kernels

115 g/4 oz low-fat curd cheese

20 g/¾ oz fresh Parmesan cheese

salt and pepper

LOW-FAT PESTO

55 g/2 oz fresh basil leaves

25 g/1 oz fresh flat-leaved parsley sprigs

NUTRITIONAL INFORMATION	
Calories	288
Protein	15g
Carbohydrate	44g
Sugars	3g
Fat	7g
Saturates	1g

variation

You could substitute pecorino – Italian ewe's milk cheese – for the Parmesan cheese, if you like.

cook's tip

If the pesto is too thick, you can dilute it with a little of the pasta cooking water, but remember to reserve the water when you drain the pasta.

1 Bring a large saucepan of lightly salted water to the boil over a medium heat. Add the pasta, return to the boil and cook for 8–10 minutes, or until tender but still firm to the bite.

2 Meanwhile, make the pesto. Place half the basil, half the parsley, the garlic, pine kernels and curd cheese in a food processor and process until smooth. Add the remaining basil and parsley, then grate and add the Parmesan cheese. Season to taste with salt and pepper. Process again briefly.

3 Drain the cooked pasta and return to the saucepan. Add the pesto to the pasta and toss thoroughly with 2 forks. Transfer to 4 large, warmed serving plates, garnish with a few sprigs of fresh basil and serve with freshly grated Parmesan cheese.

fettuccine with smoked salmon

serves 4　　　　**prep: 5 mins** ⌚　　　　**cook: 10 mins** ⌚

This simple dish takes just moments to make, looks lovely, tastes fabulous and contains absolutely no saturated fat – what more could you possibly want?

INGREDIENTS

225 g/8 oz dried fettuccine

1 tsp olive oil

1 garlic clove, finely chopped

55 g/2 oz smoked salmon, cut into thin strips

55 g/2 oz watercress leaves, plus extra to garnish

salt and pepper

NUTRITIONAL INFORMATION	
Calories	.222
Protein	.11g
Carbohydrate	.42g
Sugars	.2g
Fat	.3g
Saturates	.0g

variation

Substitute the same amount of rocket for the watercress, if you like, and garnish with a few sprigs of fresh flat-leaved parsley.

cook's tip

You can often buy misshapen offcuts of smoked salmon for a fraction of the price of neat smoked salmon slices in some large supermarkets.

1 Bring a large saucepan of lightly salted water to the boil over a medium heat. Add the pasta, return to the boil and cook for 8–10 minutes, or until tender but still firm to the bite.

2 Meanwhile, heat the olive oil in a large non-stick frying pan. Add the garlic and cook over a low heat, stirring constantly, for 30 seconds. Add the salmon and watercress, season to taste with pepper and cook for a further 30 seconds, or until the watercress has wilted.

3 Drain the cooked pasta and return to the saucepan. Mix the salmon and watercress with the pasta. Toss the mixture thoroughly using 2 large forks. Divide between 4 large serving plates and garnish with extra watercress leaves. Serve immediately.

scrumptious sandwiches

serves 1　　　　　　**prep: 5 mins** ⌛　　　　　　**cook: 0 mins** ⏱

Use your favourite type of bread or rolls, such as Granary, sourdough or rye, for these delicious sandwich fillings.

INGREDIENTS

2 slices bread or 1 roll

TUNA AND WATERCRESS FILLING

2 tbsp canned tuna in brine, drained

2 tbsp finely chopped watercress

1 tbsp canned sweetcorn, drained

2 tbsp Low-fat Mayonnaise
(see page 12)

½ tsp Dijon mustard

dash of lemon juice

salt and pepper

PRAWN AND COTTAGE CHEESE FILLING

2 tbsp low-fat cottage cheese

¼ tsp tomato purée

pepper

6 cooked, peeled prawns

1 button mushroom, thinly sliced

2–3 slices red pepper

1 fresh chive, snipped

CHICKEN FILLING

1 tbsp fat-free fromage frais

1–2 Webbs lettuce leaves, shredded

25 g/1 oz cooked chicken, skinned and cut into thin strips

¼ tsp Dijon mustard

½ celery stick, sliced

3 shelled pistachio nuts, sliced

salt and pepper

NUTRITIONAL INFORMATION	
Calories 296/250/260	
Protein 22/22/19g	
Carbohydrate 42/35/36g	
Sugars 6/5/6g	
Fat 6/3/5g	
Saturates 2/1/1g	

variation

Following the tuna recipe, replace the fish with crabmeat, the watercress with lettuce and the mustard with 1 teaspoon finely chopped fresh chilli.

cook's tip

If you are not going to eat the sandwich immediately, wrap it loosely in clingfilm or greaseproof paper and store in the refrigerator.

1 To make the tuna and watercress filling, place all the ingredients in a large bowl and, using a metal spoon, stir until thoroughly combined. Spread the tuna mixture evenly over 1 slice of bread or half a roll, then season to taste with salt and pepper and top with the remaining slice or half roll. Serve immediately.

2 To make the prawn and cottage cheese filling, place the cottage cheese in a small bowl, stir in the tomato purée and season to taste with pepper. Spread the cheese mixture over 1 slice of bread or half a roll and top with the cooked prawns and slices of mushroom and pepper. Sprinkle with the snipped chive and top with the remaining

slice of bread or half roll. Serve immediately.

3 To make the chicken filling, spread the fromage frais over 1 slice of bread or half a roll and place the lettuce on top. Toss the chicken with the mustard in a small bowl and arrange over the lettuce, then top with the celery and nuts and season

to taste with salt and pepper. Top with the remaining slice of bread or half roll.

sausage & lentil stew

serves 4   **prep: 5 mins**   **cook: 1 hr**

This warming one-pot meal is perfect for an easy light supper. Like all sausages, Spanish chorizo is high in fat, but it is so flavoursome that you require only a small quantity to liven up the lentils.

INGREDIENTS

55 g/2 oz chorizo sausage,
very thinly sliced

1 onion, finely chopped

225 g/8 oz Puy lentils

600 ml/1 pint Chicken Stock
(see page 11)

400 ml/14 fl oz water

1 carrot, thinly sliced

1 celery stick, thinly sliced

2 tsp chopped fresh parsley

salt and pepper

NUTRITIONAL INFORMATION

Calories	.217
Protein	.17g
Carbohydrate	.30g
Sugars	.3g
Fat	.4g
Saturates	.1g

cook's tip

Puy lentils are best for this stew, as they have a fine flavour and hold their shape well when cooked. You could use brown lentils instead, but red split ones would become too mushy.

1 Reserve a few slices of chorizo for the garnish and cut the remaining slices into thin strips. Dry-fry the slices and strips in a frying pan over a low heat, stirring frequently, for 2–3 minutes. Remove the chorizo slices and reserve. Add the onion to the frying pan and cook, stirring occasionally, for a further 5 minutes, or until softened.

2 Transfer the onion to a large, heavy-based saucepan. Add the lentils, Chicken Stock and water and bring to the boil over a medium heat. Cover and simmer for 30–40 minutes, or until the lentils are tender.

3 Add the carrot, celery and parsley and season to taste with salt and pepper.

Cover and simmer for a further 8–10 minutes, or until the carrot is tender. Serve immediately, garnished with the reserved chorizo slices.

sweet & sour drumsticks

cook: 20 mins

prep: 15 mins, plus 1 hr marinating

serves 4

Chicken drumsticks are marinated to impart a tangy, sweet and sour flavour and a shiny glaze before being cooked on a barbecue. They are ideal served as part of an al fresco summer party.

NUTRITIONAL INFORMATION	
Calories	171
Protein	33g
Carbohydrate	10g
Sugars	9g
Fat	5g
Saturates	1g

INGREDIENTS

8 chicken drumsticks

4 tbsp red wine vinegar

2 tbsp tomato purée

2 tbsp soy sauce

2 tbsp clear honey

1 tbsp Worcestershire sauce

1 garlic clove, finely chopped

good pinch of cayenne pepper

salt and pepper

crisp salad leaves, to serve

cook's tip

For a tangy flavour, add the juice of 1 lime to the marinade. While the drumsticks are grilling, check regularly to ensure that they are not burning.

1 Skin the chicken drumsticks, if you like and slash 2–3 times with a sharp knife. Arrange the drumsticks in a single layer in a large, non-metallic shallow dish.

2 Mix the vinegar, tomato purée, soy sauce, honey, Worcestershire sauce and garlic together in a small bowl. Season to taste with cayenne, salt and pepper, then pour the mixture over the drumsticks, turning to coat thoroughly in the marinade.

3 Cover with clingfilm and leave to marinate in the refrigerator for 1 hour. Preheat the grill to high or light a barbecue. Line a grill rack with foil and place the drumsticks on top. Cook under the grill or over hot coals for 20 minutes, brushing with the marinade during cooking, until the chicken is well browned and the juices run clear when pierced with a skewer.

4 Transfer the drumsticks to a warmed serving dish and serve immediately with crisp salad leaves.

spicy chicken with naan

serves 4 **prep: 10 mins, plus 1–2 hrs marinating** **cook: 20 mins**

This easy Indian-style dish makes a delicious lunch or supper and can be served with additional salad, if you like. It is also excellent served cold. Make mini chicken naan for children's lunch boxes.

INGREDIENTS

450 g/1 lb skinless, boneless chicken, trimmed of all visible fat and cut into 2.5-cm/1-inch cubes

4 naan breads

½ onion, sliced into rings

2 tomatoes, thinly sliced

¼ iceberg lettuce, shredded

MARINADE

3 tbsp low-fat natural yogurt

1 tsp garam masala

1 tsp chilli powder

2 tbsp lime juice

2 tbsp chopped fresh coriander

1 fresh red chilli, deseeded and finely chopped

salt and pepper

NUTRITIONAL INFORMATION

Calories	503
Protein	42g
Carbohydrate	72g
Sugars	6g
Fat	15g
Saturates	3g

variation

You could serve the chicken and salad in pitta pockets, if you like. Toast the pitta breads lightly first, then cut a slit with a sharp knife to make a pocket.

cook's tip

To make the chicken less spicy, use just ¼ teaspoon of garam masala and ¼ teaspoon of chilli powder and omit the fresh chilli in the marinade.

1 Place the chicken cubes in a shallow, non-metallic dish. Place all the marinade ingredients in a jug and stir until well blended, seasoning to taste with salt and pepper. Pour the marinade over the chicken, tossing to coat thoroughly. Cover with clingfilm and leave to marinate in the refrigerator for 1–2 hours.

2 Preheat the grill to high. Using a slotted spoon, transfer the chicken to a flameproof dish and cook under the preheated hot grill, stirring occasionally, for 20 minutes, or until tender and cooked through.

3 Meanwhile, cut a slit in the naan breads to make a pocket. Fill the naan pockets with the cooked chicken, onion rings, tomato slices and shredded lettuce and serve immediately.

minty lamb burgers

⏲ **cook: 20 mins**

🕐 **prep: 15 mins,
plus 1 hr 30 mins chilling**

serves 4

NUTRITIONAL INFORMATION	
Calories	320
Protein	28g
Carbohydrate	33g
Sugars	11g
Fat	10g
Saturates	4g

variation

If you have a limited amount of time, replace the dressing with shop-bought tomato relish or mango chutney.

A delicious alternative to traditional hamburgers, these low-fat lamb burgers are flavoured with chopped fresh mint and are accompanied with a smooth minty dressing.

INGREDIENTS

350 g/12 oz lean lamb mince

1 medium onion, finely chopped

4 tbsp dry wholemeal breadcrumbs

2 tbsp mint jelly

salt and pepper

TO SERVE

4 wholemeal baps, split

2 large tomatoes, sliced

small piece of cucumber, sliced

lettuce leaves

DRESSING

4 tbsp low-fat natural fromage frais

1 tbsp mint jelly, softened

5-cm/2-inch piece cucumber, finely diced

1 tbsp chopped fresh mint

cook's tip

To cook on a preheated barbecue, place the burgers on a grill rack and cook for 8 minutes, turn over and cook for 7 minutes, or until cooked through. Keep turning to stop them drying out and burning.

1 Place the lamb in a large bowl and mix in the onion, breadcrumbs and mint jelly. Season well with salt and pepper, then mould the ingredients together with your hands to form a firm mixture.

2 Divide the mixture into 4 portions and form each portion into a round measuring 10 cm/4 inches

across. Place the rounds on a plate lined with baking paper and leave to chill in the refrigerator for 30 minutes.

3 Preheat the grill to medium. Line a grill rack with baking paper, securing the ends under the rack, and place the burgers on top. Cook for 8 minutes, then turn the burgers over with a

spatula and cook for a further 7 minutes, or until the burgers are cooked through.

4 Meanwhile, make the dressing. Mix the fromage frais, mint jelly, cucumber and chopped mint together in a small bowl. Cover with clingfilm and leave to chill in the refrigerator for 1 hour, or until required. Drain the

burgers on kitchen paper and serve inside baps with sliced tomatoes, cucumber, lettuce and the dressing.

turkey patties

serves 4

prep: 15 mins, plus 30 mins chilling

cook: 20–25 mins

These savoury patties are served with a colourful beetroot and apple sauce that gives a fabulous boost to the sometimes bland flavour of turkey. The sauce would taste just as good with plain grilled or griddled turkey breasts.

INGREDIENTS

1½ tsp sunflower or corn oil

55 g/2 oz fresh spinach, shredded

2 garlic cloves, finely chopped

225 g/8 oz skinless, boneless turkey breast, trimmed of all visible fat and finely chopped

6 tbsp cold mashed potato

175 g/6 oz low-fat cottage cheese, strained

3 spring onions, chopped

1 tsp wholegrain mustard

2 tbsp chopped fresh basil

40 g/1½ oz dried breadcrumbs

salt and pepper

fresh dill sprigs, to garnish

SAUCE

1 peeled, cooked beetroot, finely diced

300 ml/10 fl oz apple purée or unsweetened apple sauce

1 tsp Dijon mustard

1 tsp snipped fresh dill

NUTRITIONAL INFORMATION

Calories	.215
Protein	.22g
Carbohydrate	.26g
Sugars	.10g
Fat	.3g
Saturates	.1g

variation

If you are planning to cook the beetroot for the sauce yourself, you could use the green tops as a substitute for the spinach.

cook's tip

Dampen your hands slightly before forming the mixture into patties to prevent it sticking to your fingers. To make coating easier, place the breadcrumbs on a plate and roll the patties in them.

1 Preheat the oven to 190°C/375°F/Gas Mark 5. To make the sauce, mix all the ingredients together in a bowl, cover with clingfilm and leave to chill in the refrigerator until required. Alternatively, place all the ingredients in a food processor and process until smooth, then transfer to a small bowl, cover and chill in the refrigerator until required.

2 To make the patties, heat the oil in a non-stick frying pan. Add the spinach and garlic, then cover and cook over a low heat for 2 minutes, or until the spinach has wilted. Remove from the heat and leave to cool. When cool, place in a bowl and mix with the turkey, potato, cottage cheese, spring onions, mustard, basil and half the breadcrumbs. Season to taste with salt and pepper. Form the mixture into 8 patties, about 1 cm/½ inch thick. Coat with the remaining breadcrumbs.

3 Place the patties on a baking tray and bake in the preheated oven for 15–20 minutes, or until golden brown. Transfer to 4 warmed serving plates, add a spoonful of sauce to each plate and top with a fresh dill sprig. Serve immediately.

roast summer vegetables

serves 4   **prep: 10 mins** ⟳   **cook: 20–25 mins** ⟳

*This appetizing and colourful mixture of Mediterranean vegetables
makes a sensational summer lunch for vegetarians and meat-eaters
alike. Roasting brings out the full flavour and sweetness of the
peppers, aubergines, courgettes and onions.*

INGREDIENTS

2 tbsp olive oil	1 orange pepper
1 fennel bulb	4 garlic cloves
2 red onions	4 fresh rosemary sprigs
2 beef tomatoes	pepper
1 aubergine	crusty bread, to serve (optional)
2 courgettes	
1 yellow pepper	
1 red pepper	

NUTRITIONAL INFORMATION

Calories	142
Protein	. . . . .4g
Carbohydrate	. . . . .18g
Sugars	. . . . .13g
Fat	. . . . .7g
Saturates	. . . . .1g

variation

Substitute a herb-flavoured oil, such
as tarragon or garlic and rosemary,
for the plain olive oil, if you like.

cook's tip

You can also serve this dish as
an accompaniment to grilled
or barbecued chicken or
monkfish. This quantity will
serve 8 people.

1 Preheat the oven
to 200°C/400°F/Gas
Mark 6. Brush a large
ovenproof dish with a little of
the olive oil. Prepare the
vegetables. Cut the fennel,
red onions and tomatoes into
wedges. Slice the aubergine
and courgettes thickly, then
deseed all the peppers and
cut into chunks. Arrange the
vegetables in the dish and

tuck the garlic cloves and
rosemary sprigs among them.
Drizzle with the remaining
olive oil and season to taste
with pepper.

2 Roast in the preheated
oven for 10 minutes.
Remove the dish from the oven
and turn the vegetables over
with a slotted spoon. Return to
the oven and roast for a

further 10–15 minutes, or
until tender and beginning to
turn golden brown.

3 Serve the vegetables
straight from the dish,
or transfer to a warmed
serving plate. Serve with crusty
bread, if you like.

mexican eggs

serves 4   **prep: 10 mins**   **cook: 50 mins**

This dish is simple to prepare and makes the perfect lunch or light supper. Serve straight from the frying pan with plenty of crisp salad or a selection of freshly steamed vegetables, if you like.

INGREDIENTS

1 tbsp sunflower or corn oil	1 tsp ground cumin
1 red pepper, deseeded and cut into batons	125 ml/4 fl oz red wine
1 yellow pepper, deseeded and cut into batons	800 g/1 lb 12 oz canned chopped tomatoes
1 garlic clove, finely chopped	1 tsp muscovado sugar
2 fresh red chillies, deseeded and finely chopped	salt and pepper
1 tsp ground coriander	4 eggs
	2 tbsp chopped fresh coriander, to garnish

NUTRITIONAL INFORMATION	
Calories	156
Protein	8g
Carbohydrate	7g
Sugars	7g
Fat	8g
Saturates	2g

variation

If you like, omit the chillies and add 115 g/4 oz thinly sliced mushrooms and 225 g/8 oz canned sweetcorn with the tomatoes in Step 2.

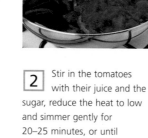

cook's tip

Capsaicin – the substance that makes chillies hot – is not found in the seeds, but is concentrated in the flesh surrounding them. Removing the seeds will reduce the heat.

1 Heat the sunflower oil in a large frying pan. Add the peppers and garlic and cook over a medium heat, stirring occasionally, for 2 minutes, or until softened. Stir in the chillies, ground coriander and cumin and cook, stirring, for 1 minute. Pour in the red wine, bring to the boil, reduce the heat to medium and simmer for 3 minutes.

2 Stir in the tomatoes with their juice and the sugar, reduce the heat to low and simmer gently for 20–25 minutes, or until thickened. Season to taste with salt and pepper.

3 Using a large spoon, make 4 hollows in the tomato mixture. Break an egg into each hollow, cover the frying pan and cook for 10–15 minutes, or until set. Sprinkle with chopped fresh coriander and serve.

soufflé omelette

serves 4 **prep: 15 mins** **cook: 45 mins**

The combination of sweet cherry tomatoes, mixed mushrooms and peppery rocket leaves make a mouthwatering filling for these very light, fluffy omelettes.

INGREDIENTS

175 g/6 oz cherry tomatoes

225 g/8 oz mixed mushrooms, such as button, shiitake and oyster mushrooms

4 tbsp Vegetable Stock (see page 11)

small bunch of fresh thyme

salt and pepper

4 medium eggs, separated

8 tbsp water

4 medium egg whites

4 tsp olive oil

25 g/1 oz rocket leaves

fresh thyme sprigs, to garnish

NUTRITIONAL INFORMATION	
Calories	146
Protein	. . . . .10g
Carbohydrate	. . . . .2g
Sugars	. . . . .2g
Fat	. . . . .11g
Saturates	. . . . .2g

cook's tip

When whisking egg whites, make sure the bowl is spotlessly clean and free from grease, otherwise the egg whites will lose their shape.

1 Preheat the grill to medium. Halve the tomatoes and place them in a large saucepan. Wipe the mushrooms with kitchen paper, trim if necessary and slice if large, then place them in the saucepan.

2 Add the Vegetable Stock and thyme to the saucepan. Bring to the boil,

cover and simmer for 5–6 minutes, or until tender. Drain, remove and discard the thyme and season to taste with salt and pepper. Keep warm.

3 Meanwhile, separate the eggs. Whisk the egg yolks with the water until frothy. Whisk the 8 egg whites in a spotlessly clean, greasefree bowl until stiff and dry.

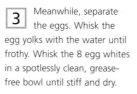

4 Spoon the egg yolk mixture into the egg whites and, using a metal spoon, fold together until well mixed. Take care not to knock out too much of the air. Brush a small omelette pan with 1 teaspoon of olive oil and heat until hot. Pour in onequarter of the egg mixture and cook for 4–5 minutes, or until the mixture has set. Finish

cooking the omelette under the preheated hot grill for 2–3 minutes. Transfer to a warmed serving plate and keep warm while cooking the remaining omelettes. Fill the omelettes with a few rocket leaves, and one-quarter of the mushroom mixture. Flip over the top, garnish with a few sprigs of thyme and serve.

breakfast muffins

cook: 25 mins | **prep: 20 mins** | **serves 4**

Try this tasty and very filling breakfast or brunch – a lightly toasted wholemeal muffin, topped with lean bacon rashers, grilled tomato, mushrooms and a poached egg.

NUTRITIONAL INFORMATION	
Calories	159
Protein	12g
Carbohydrate	12g
Sugars	1g
Fat	7g
Saturates	20g

INGREDIENTS

2 wholemeal muffins

8 lean back bacon rashers, rinds removed

4 medium eggs

2 large tomatoes

salt and pepper

2 large flat mushrooms

4 tbsp Vegetable Stock (see page 11)

1 small bunch of fresh chives, snipped, to garnish

(see page 11)

variation

Omit the bacon for a vegetarian version and use more tomatoes and mushrooms instead. Alternatively, include a grilled low-fat tofu burger.

1 Preheat the grill to medium. Cut the muffins in half and lightly toast them under the hot grill for 1–2 minutes on the open side. Transfer to a warmed plate and keep warm.

2 Using a sharp knife, trim off all visible fat from the bacon and cook under the preheated hot grill for 2–3 minutes on each side, until cooked through. Drain on kitchen paper and keep warm.

3 Place 4 egg-poaching rings in a frying pan, then pour in enough water to cover the base of the frying pan. Bring to the boil and reduce the heat to a simmer. Break 1 egg into each ring and cook for 6 minutes, or until set.

4 Cut the tomatoes into 8 thick slices and arrange on foil on a grill rack. Grill under the preheated hot grill for 2–3 minutes, or until just cooked. Season to taste with salt and pepper. Peel and thickly slice the mushrooms. Place in a saucepan with the Vegetable Stock, bring to the boil, cover and simmer for 4–5 minutes. Drain and keep warm. Arrange the tomato and mushroom slices on the toasted muffins and top each with 2 bacon rashers. Carefully place a poached egg on top of each and sprinkle with a little pepper. Garnish with snipped fresh chives and serve.

rice & tuna peppers

cook: 35 mins   **prep: 10 mins**   serves 4

Grilled mixed sweet peppers are filled with tender tuna, sweetcorn, nutty brown and wild rice and grated, reduced-fat cheese. Serve with a large crisp salad to make a filling lunch.

INGREDIENTS

55 g/2 oz wild rice

55 g/2 oz brown rice

4 assorted medium peppers

200 g/7 oz canned tuna fish in brine, drained and flaked

325 g/11½ oz canned sweetcorn kernels (with no added sugar or salt), drained

100 g/3½ oz reduced-fat mature Cheddar cheese, grated

1 bunch of fresh basil leaves, shredded

salt and pepper

2 tbsp dry white breadcrumbs

1 tbsp freshly grated Parmesan cheese

fresh basil leaves, to garnish

crisp salad leaves, to serve

variation

If you want to reduce the fat content in this dish further, then omit the Cheddar cheese and only use a little Parmesan cheese.

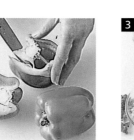

cook's tip

When cooking peppers under the grill, make sure the grill rack is lined with foil to catch any juices. Keep a close eye on them as they can burn.

1 Preheat the grill to medium. Place the wild rice and brown rice in different saucepans, cover with water and cook for 15 minutes, or according to the packet instructions. Drain thoroughly and reserve until required.

2 Meanwhile, halve the peppers, remove the seeds and stalks and arrange the peppers on a grill rack, cut-side down. Cook under the hot grill for 5 minutes, turn over and cook for 4–5 minutes.

 Transfer the rice to a large bowl and add the tuna and sweetcorn. Gently fold in the grated cheese. Stir the basil leaves into the rice mixture and season to taste with salt and pepper.

4 Divide the tuna and rice mixture into 8 equal portions, then pile each portion into each cooked pepper half. Mix the breadcrumbs and Parmesan cheese together in a bowl and sprinkle over each pepper. Place the peppers under the preheated hot grill and cook for 4–5 minutes, or until hot and golden brown. Transfer the peppers to a large serving plate, garnish with fresh basil leaves and serve immediately with a crisp salad.

mushroom risotto

serves 4
prep: 10 mins, ↺
plus 30 mins soaking
cook: 30 mins ⏱

To achieve the authentic creamy texture of risotto, use arborio or carnaroli rice. These shorter-grain varieties can absorb more liquid than long-grain rice, but still retain their 'bite'. They are widely available from supermarkets and may be labelled 'risotto rice'. Avoid easy-cook risotto rice, which will not have the same texture.

INGREDIENTS

15 g/½ oz dried porcini mushrooms

300 ml/10 fl oz boiling water

1 tbsp olive oil

1 onion, finely chopped

1 garlic clove, finely chopped

1 fresh sage sprig, finely chopped

300 g/10½ oz risotto rice

125 ml/4 fl oz white wine

225 g/8 oz chestnut mushrooms, sliced

700 ml/1¼ pints hot Vegetable Stock (see page 11)

4 tbsp freshly grated Parmesan cheese

salt and pepper

shavings of fresh Parmesan cheese, to garnish

NUTRITIONAL INFORMATION	
Calories	.384
Protein	.10g
Carbohydrate	.71g
Sugars	.2g
Fat	.7g
Saturates	.2g

variation

Instead of chestnut mushrooms, use field mushrooms. Substitute Chicken Stock (see page 11) for Vegetable Stock, if you like.

cook's tip

Place the stock in a separate saucepan before you begin cooking the risotto. Bring to the boil, then reduce the heat and simmer to keep the stock at the right temperature while you add it to the rice.

1 Place the dried porcini mushrooms in a small bowl and pour in the boiling water to cover. Leave to soak for 30 minutes, or until the mushrooms are soft. Drain, reserving the soaking liquid. Using a sharp knife, chop the mushrooms and sieve the soaking liquid through a coffee filter paper or muslin-lined sieve.

2 Heat the olive oil in a large, heavy-based saucepan. Add the onion, garlic and sage and cook, stirring frequently, for 5 minutes. Add the rice and cook over a low heat, stirring constantly to coat the grains with the oil, for 3 minutes. Add the wine and cook, stirring constantly, until it has evaporated. Stir in the porcini and chestnut mushrooms, the mushroom soaking liquid and a large ladleful of the hot Vegetable Stock. Simmer, stirring constantly, until all the stock has been absorbed. Continue adding stock and stirring in this way for 20 minutes, or until all the stock has been absorbed and the rice is tender but still firm to the bite.

3 Remove the saucepan from the heat, stir in the Parmesan cheese and season to taste with salt and pepper. Divide the risotto between 4 warmed serving plates, garnish with shavings of Parmesan cheese and serve.

cheesy ham savoury

serves 4   **prep: 10 mins** ⟲   **cook: 7 mins** ⟰

Lean ham wrapped around crisp celery, topped with a light crust of cheese and spring onions, makes a delicious light lunch. Serve with a fresh tomato salad and crusty bread.

INGREDIENTS

4 celery sticks

12 thin slices of lean ham

1 bunch of spring onions

celery salt and pepper

175 g/6 oz low-fat soft cheese with garlic and herbs

6 tbsp low-fat natural yogurt

4 tbsp freshly grated Parmesan cheese

TO SERVE

tomato salad

crusty bread

NUTRITIONAL INFORMATION

Calories	188
Protein	15g
Carbohydrate	5g
Sugars	5g
Fat	12g
Saturates	7g

cook's tip

Parmesan cheese is useful in low-fat recipes because its intense flavour means you need to use only a very small amount.

1 Preheat the grill to medium. Wash the celery under cold running water, then remove any leaves and discard. Slice each celery stick into 3 equal portions. Cut any visible fat off the ham and lay the slices on a chopping board. Place a portion of celery on each piece of ham and roll up. Place 3 rolls in each of 4 small, heatproof dishes.

2 Trim the spring onions, then finely shred both the white and green parts. Sprinkle the spring onions over the rolls and season to taste with celery salt and pepper.

3 Mix the soft cheese and yogurt together in a small bowl, then spoon the mixture over the rolls. Sprinkle each portion with 1 tablespoon of freshly grated Parmesan cheese and cook under the preheated hot grill for 6–7 minutes, or until hot and the cheese has formed a crust. If the cheese begins to brown too quickly, reduce the temperature. Serve immediately with a tomato salad and crusty bread.

baked potatoes with pesto chicken

⏲ **cook: 1 hr–1 hr 15 mins**   ⏱ **prep: 5 mins**   **serves 4**

Filled baked potatoes make wonderful comfort food on a cold day, but resist the urge to add butter, soured cream or grated cheese. This dish needs only a green salad to make a delicious light meal.

NUTRITIONAL INFORMATION	
Calories	250
Protein	20g
Carbohydrate	31g
Sugars	6g
Fat	6g
Saturates	1g

INGREDIENTS

4 large potatoes

sunflower or corn oil, for brushing

2 skinless, boneless chicken breasts, about 115 g/4 oz each, trimmed of all visible fat

250 ml/9 fl oz low-fat natural yogurt

1 tbsp Low-fat Pesto (see page 58)

green salad, to serve

cook's tip

If you do not have a griddle pan, cook the chicken under a preheated hot grill instead, but leave the skin on to prevent the flesh from drying out. Remove the skin before slicing the chicken.

1 Preheat the oven to 200°C/400°F/Gas Mark 6. Prick the potatoes all over with a fork and bake in the preheated oven for 1–1¼ hours, or until soft and cooked through.

2 About 15 minutes before the potatoes are ready, heat a griddle pan and brush with a little sunflower oil. Add the chicken and cook over a medium–high heat for 5 minutes on each side, or until cooked through and tender. Meanwhile, place the yogurt and pesto in a bowl and mix until blended.

3 Slice the potatoes down the centre, almost right through, and open out. Cut the cooked chicken into slices.

Divide the slices between the potatoes and top with the yogurt. Transfer to 4 warmed serving plates and serve with a green salad.

potato & tuna quiche

cook: 1 hr   **prep: 20 mins**   **serves 4**

variation

To make a vegetarian version, replace the tuna with 1 bunch of cooked asparagus spears arranged over the top. Proceed as in main recipe.

The base for this quiche is made from mashed potato instead of pastry, giving a softer textured case for the tasty tuna filling.

INGREDIENTS

450 g/1 lb floury potatoes, peeled and diced

25 g/1 oz butter

6 tbsp plain flour, plus extra for dusting

FILLING

1 tbsp vegetable oil

1 shallot, chopped

1 garlic clove, crushed

1 red pepper, diced

175g/6 oz canned tuna in brine, drained

50 g/1¾ oz canned sweetcorn, drained

150 ml/5 fl oz skimmed milk

3 eggs, beaten

1 tbsp chopped fresh dill

salt and pepper

50 g/1¾ oz mature low-fat Cheddar cheese, grated

fresh dill sprigs, to garnish

TO SERVE

lemon wedges

shredded celery

cook's tip

Place the flan tin on a large baking sheet before baking in the oven. This makes it much easier to handle and will also catch any drips.

 1 Preheat the oven to 200°C/400°F/Gas Mark 6. Cook the potatoes in a saucepan of boiling water for 10 minutes, or until tender.

2 Drain the potatoes and mash well. Add the butter and flour and mix to form a dough. Turn the dough out on to a lightly floured work surface and knead, then press into a 20-cm/8-inch flan tin. Prick the base with a fork and line with baking paper and baking beans. Bake blind in the preheated oven for 20 minutes.

3 Heat the vegetable oil in a frying pan, add the shallot, garlic and pepper and fry gently over a low heat for 5 minutes. Drain thoroughly and spoon the mixture into the cooked flan case. Flake the tuna and arrange it over the top with the sweetcorn.

4 Mix the milk and beaten eggs together in a bowl, then mix in the chopped dill. Season to taste with salt and pepper, then pour over the tuna and sweetcorn. Sprinkle over the grated cheese and bake in the preheated oven for 20 minutes, or until the filling has set. Garnish with fresh dill sprigs and serve with lemon wedges and shredded celery.

vegetable samosas

serves 4 **prep: 30 mins** **cook: 35–40 mins**

Everyone will love these hot and spicy vegetable samosas as they are oven-baked rather than deep-fried. Serve either hot or cold with mango chutney as a starter or as part of a light lunch. They are also perfect as a snack at any time of the day.

INGREDIENTS

1 small potato, peeled and quartered
1 small carrot, halved
4 cauliflower florets
1 tsp sunflower or corn oil, plus extra for brushing
2 tsp lime juice
1 tbsp water
1 shallot, finely chopped
3 tbsp frozen peas
1 fresh green chilli, deseeded and finely chopped
½ tsp cumin seeds

½ tsp black mustard seeds
½ tsp ground turmeric
½ tsp ground coriander
beaten egg, to glaze
mango chutney, to serve

PASTRY
40 g/1½ oz malted flour
125 g/4½ oz plain flour, plus extra for dusting
40 g/1½ oz sunflower margarine
50–75 ml/2–2½ fl oz skimmed milk

NUTRITIONAL INFORMATION

Calories	139
Protein	. . . . .4g
Carbohydrate	. . . . .19g
Sugars	. . . . .2g
Fat	. . . . .6g
Saturates	. . . . .2g

variation

If you would like these samosas to taste a little spicier, use 2 fresh green chillies, deseeded and finely chopped, instead of just one.

cook's tip

If you have time, wrap the dough in foil and leave to chill in the refrigerator for 15–30 minutes before you roll it out.

1 Preheat the oven to 190°C/375°F/Gas Mark 5. Cook the potato, carrot and cauliflower in a small saucepan of boiling water for 10 minutes. Drain, leave to cool slightly, then chop. Place the oil, lime juice, water, shallot, peas, chilli and spices in a small pan, bring to the boil, then reduce the heat and simmer gently, stirring occasionally, for 3 minutes. Stir in the potato, carrot and cauliflower and transfer to a bowl to cool.

2 To make the pastry, sift the flours into a bowl, add the margarine and rub it in with your fingertips until the mixture resembles breadcrumbs. Add just enough milk to make a firm dough.

Turn out on to a lightly floured work surface and knead gently until smooth. Divide the dough into 4 equal pieces and roll each out into an 18-cm/ 7-inch round. Trim the edges and cut each round in half.

3 Brush a baking sheet with a little sunflower oil. Divide the vegetable mixture between the dough semi-circles, placing it on one half only and leaving a small border. Brush the edges with water, fold the dough over and seal, pressing the edges together. Brush with beaten egg, transfer to the baking sheet and bake in the oven for 20–25 minutes, or until golden brown. Serve hot or cold with mango chutney.

layered vegetable bake

serves 4   **prep: 10 mins** ⏲   **cook: 1 hr 30 mins** ⏲

Simplicity itself, this tasty bake makes a superb meal in itself or can be served as a vegetable accompaniment to griddled chicken, in which case it will serve 8 people.

INGREDIENTS

1 tbsp olive oil, for brushing

675 g/1 lb 8 oz potatoes

2 leeks

2 beef tomatoes

8 fresh basil leaves

1 garlic clove, finely chopped

300 ml/10 fl oz Vegetable Stock (see page 11)

salt and pepper

NUTRITIONAL INFORMATION	
Calories	174
Protein	.5g
Carbohydrate	33g
Sugars	4g
Fat	4g
Saturates	1g

variation

You could add 2 thinly sliced courgettes to the layers of leeks for an even more substantial supper dish.

1 Preheat the oven to 180°C/350°F/Gas Mark 4. Brush a large ovenproof dish with a little of the olive oil. Prepare all the vegetables. Peel and thinly slice the potatoes, trim and slice the leeks and slice the tomatoes. Place a layer of potato slices in the base of the dish, sprinkle with half the basil leaves and cover with a layer of leeks. Top with a layer of tomato slices. Repeat these layers until all the vegetables are used up, ending with a layer of potatoes.

2 Stir the garlic into the Vegetable Stock and season to taste with salt and pepper. Pour the stock over the vegetables and brush the top with the remaining olive oil.

3 Bake in the preheated oven for 1½ hours, or until the vegetables are tender and the topping is golden brown. Serve immediately.

cottage potatoes

cook: 1 hr   **prep: 10 mins**   **serves 4**

Give the humble potato a surprising kick with this delicious spiced cheese filling. Serve with a tomato and onion salad or on a bed of colourful mixed salad leaves.

NUTRITIONAL INFORMATION	
Calories	211
Protein	11g
Carbohydrate	29g
Sugars	3g
Fat	6g
Saturates	1g

INGREDIENTS

4 baking potatoes

2 tsp sun-dried tomato purée

½ tsp ground coriander

salt and pepper

1 tbsp olive oil

3–4 spring onions, finely chopped

1–2 fresh green chillies, deseeded and finely chopped

1 tbsp tequila

1 tbsp finely chopped fresh coriander

225 g/8 oz low-fat cottage cheese

fresh coriander sprigs, to garnish

lime wedges, to serve

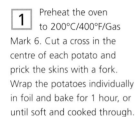

cook's tip

To cook the potatoes in the microwave, prick with a fork and place on kitchen paper. Cook on High for 6 minutes, turn over and cook for a further 8 minutes.

1 Preheat the oven to 200°C/400°F/Gas Mark 6. Cut a cross in the centre of each potato and prick the skins with a fork. Wrap the potatoes individually in foil and bake for 1 hour, or until soft and cooked through.

2 Meanwhile, mix the sun-dried tomato purée and ground coriander together in a small bowl. Season to taste with salt and pepper. Just before the potatoes are ready, heat the olive oil in a small saucepan and add the spring onions and chopped chillies. Cook, stirring occasionally, for 2–3 minutes, or until softened. Stir in the sun-dried tomato paste mixture and tequila and cook for a further 1 minute. Remove from the heat and stir in the chopped coriander. Place the cottage cheese in a bowl and stir in the tomato mixture. Blend thoroughly.

3 Unwrap the potatoes and squeeze gently to open out the cut side. Divide the cottage cheese mixture equally among the potatoes and garnish with coriander. Serve with lime wedges.

falafel

makes 24

prep: 15 mins,
plus 1 hr chilling

cook: 2 hrs

These scrumptious Middle Eastern morsels are a must-have on a buffet table and are ideal snacks for any time of day. Traditionally they are deep-fried, but here they are oven-baked and served with a spicy yogurt dip to counteract the slightly drier texture.

INGREDIENTS

225 g/8 oz dried chickpeas, soaked overnight and drained

1 onion, chopped

2 garlic cloves, chopped

2 tsp cumin seeds

2 tsp ground coriander

2 tbsp chopped fresh parsley

2 tbsp chopped fresh coriander

salt and pepper

sunflower or corn oil, for brushing

DIP

150 ml/5 fl oz low-fat natural yogurt

1 tbsp chopped fresh coriander

1 tbsp chopped fresh mint

2 tsp grated onion

1 fresh red chilli, deseeded and finely chopped

¼ tsp ground cumin

dash of lemon juice

NUTRITIONAL INFORMATION

Calories	.42
Protein	.3g
Carbohydrate	.6g
Sugars	.1g
Fat	.1g
Saturates	.0g

variation

If time is limited use 225 g/8 oz canned chickpeas instead of the dried. Replace the yogurt with fat-free fromage frais for a thicker dip.

cook's tip

When cooking dried chickpeas, skim off any scum that rises to the surface during cooking with a slotted spoon and always season after they have been cooked, otherwise they will become tough.

1 Place the chickpeas in a saucepan, cover with water and bring to the boil over a medium heat. Cook for 1–1½ hours, or until tender, then drain. Place the chickpeas, onion, garlic, cumin seeds, ground coriander, parsley and fresh coriander in a food processor and process until a firm paste forms. Transfer to a bowl, season to taste with salt and pepper, cover with clingfilm and chill in the refrigerator for 1 hour.

2 To make the dip, mix all the ingredients together in a bowl, cover and chill in the refrigerator until required.

3 Preheat the oven to 200°C/400°F/Gas Mark 6. Brush a baking sheet with sunflower oil. Using your hands, form the chickpea mixture into walnut-sized balls, place on the baking sheet and flatten them slightly. Brush with sunflower oil and bake in the preheated hot oven for 15 minutes. Turn over and bake for a further 15 minutes, or until brown. Serve warm with the dip.

poor man's tomatoes

serves 4 | **prep: 20 mins** | **cook: 35 mins**

These elegantly filled tomatoes are perfect for any occasion, whether they are used for a family supper or as a starter for a dinner party. They are ideal served with a fresh, crisp salad.

INGREDIENTS

4 large tomatoes

2 tbsp finely chopped fresh basil

4 tsp olive oil

280 g/10 oz button mushrooms, very finely chopped

1 small onion, very finely chopped

2 garlic cloves, very finely chopped

1 tablespoon chopped fresh parsley

salt and pepper

225 ml/8 fl oz Vegetable Stock (see page 11)

1 tbsp freshly grated Parmesan cheese

fresh basil sprigs, to garnish

NUTRITIONAL INFORMATION

Calories	78
Protein	3g
Carbohydrate	6g
Sugars	6g
Fat	5g
Saturates	1g

variation

To fill peppers, cut the tops off and remove the seeds. Blanch in boiling water for 2 minutes. Drain. Add 4 chopped tomatoes to the stuffing.

1 Preheat the oven to 180°C/350°F/Gas Mark 4. Slice a 'lid' from the top of each tomato and reserve. Using a teaspoon, carefully scoop out the flesh from the tomato shells and chop. Place it in a small bowl and add 1 teaspoon of the chopped fresh basil. Invert the tomato shells on kitchen paper to drain.

2 Heat 3 teaspoons of the olive oil in a frying pan. Add the mushrooms, onion, garlic, parsley and remaining basil and season to taste with pepper. Cover and cook over a low heat for 2 minutes, then remove the lid and cook, stirring occasionally, for a further 8–10 minutes. Meanwhile, bring the stock to the boil and cook until reduced by three-quarters. Stir in the tomato mixture and cook for a further 3–4 minutes, or until thickened. Rub the mixture through a sieve with a wooden spoon and stir it into the mushroom mixture. Stir in the Parmesan cheese.

3 Stand the tomatoes, the right way up, in an ovenproof dish and season the insides with salt. Divide the stuffing mixture between them and replace the 'lids'. Brush with the remaining olive oil and bake in the preheated oven for 15 minutes, or until tender and cooked through. Garnish with a few sprigs of fresh basil and serve warm.

corn & pepper pancakes

⏲ **cook: 20 mins**   ⏱ **prep: 15 mins**   **serves 4**

These light-as-air pancakes are very moreish, so it's fortunate that they are so easy to make. For best results, use a heavy-based frying pan or griddle pan, preferably one with a non-stick lining.

NUTRITIONAL INFORMATION	
Calories	239
Protein	8g
Carbohydrate	40g
Sugars	3g
Fat	6g
Saturates	1g

INGREDIENTS

150 g/5½ oz frozen sweetcorn
kernels, thawed
4 tbsp cornmeal
4 tbsp plain flour
1 small red pepper, deseeded and
very finely chopped
1 small egg yolk
½ tsp caster sugar
2 egg whites
1 tbsp olive oil

variation

You can use the same quantity of fresh sweetcorn as canned, in which case, you will require 1 large cob.

1 Place half the sweetcorn kernels in a food processor and process until finely chopped. Place the remaining sweetcorn kernels, cornmeal, flour and chopped pepper in a bowl and add the processed sweetcorn. Beat the egg yolk with the sugar in a separate small bowl, then add it to the sweetcorn mixture and stir thoroughly.

2 Beat the egg whites in a spotlessly clean, greasefree bowl until they stand in soft peaks. Gently fold half the egg whites into the sweetcorn mixture, then fold in the remaining egg whites.

3 Heat half the olive oil in a heavy-based frying pan. Drop spoonfuls of the batter into the frying pan, spacing them well apart, and cook for 3 minutes, or until the undersides are golden brown. Flip over carefully with a spatula and cook the other sides for 3 minutes, or until golden brown. Transfer to a warmed serving plate and keep warm while you cook the remaining pancakes, adding more oil, if necessary. Serve immediately.

pasta niçoise salad

serves 4 **prep: 15 mins** ⟳ **cook: 35 mins** ⟳

*Based on the classic French salad niçoise, this recipe has a
light olive oil dressing with the tang of capers and the fragrance
of fresh basil.*

INGREDIENTS

225 g/8 oz dried farfalle

salt and pepper

175 g/6 oz French beans,
topped and tailed

350 g/12 oz fresh tuna steaks

115 g/4 oz baby plum tomatoes, halved

8 anchovy fillets, drained on
kitchen paper

2 tbsp capers in brine, drained

25 g/1 oz stoned black olives
in brine, drained

fresh basil leaves, to garnish

DRESSING

1 tbsp olive oil

1 garlic clove, crushed

1 tbsp lemon juice

½ tsp finely grated lemon rind

1 tbsp shredded fresh basil leaves

<table>
<tr><td colspan="2">NUTRITIONAL INFORMATION</td></tr>
<tr><td>Calories</td><td>.214</td></tr>
<tr><td>Protein</td><td>.26g</td></tr>
<tr><td>Carbohydrate</td><td>.14g</td></tr>
<tr><td>Sugars</td><td>.2g</td></tr>
<tr><td>Fat</td><td>.7g</td></tr>
<tr><td>Saturates</td><td>.1g</td></tr>
</table>

variation

Any pasta shape is suitable for this
salad – to make it even more
colourful, use tricolour pasta.

cook's tip

Dried pasta will keep for
6 months. Once opened, the
packet should be resealed or
the pasta should be kept in
an airtight jar.

 1 Preheat the grill to
medium. Cook the
pasta in a large, heavy-based
saucepan of lightly salted
boiling water according to the
packet instructions, or until
just tender but still firm to the
bite. Drain, return to the
saucepan and keep warm.

2 Cook the French beans
in a small saucepan of
lightly salted boiling water for
5–6 minutes, or until just
tender. Drain well and toss into
the pasta. Keep warm.

3 Rinse the tuna under
cold running water and
pat dry on kitchen paper.
Season on both sides with
pepper. Place the tuna on
a grill rack and cook for
4–5 minutes on each side, or

until cooked through. Drain the
tuna on kitchen paper and,
using a knife and fork, flake
into bite-sized pieces. Toss the
tuna into the pasta together
with the tomatoes, anchovies,
capers and olives. Reserve and
keep warm.

 4 Meanwhile, prepare the
dressing. Mix all the
ingredients together in a small

bowl and season well with salt
and pepper. Pour the dressing
over the pasta mixture and mix
carefully. Transfer to a warmed
serving bowl and garnish with
fresh basil leaves. Serve.

mackerel & potato salad

serves 4　　　　**prep: 25 mins,**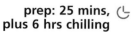
plus 6 hrs chilling　　　　**cook: 10 mins**

Inexpensive and packed with flavour, mackerel is an ideal fish to use in salads. In this recipe, it is combined with nutty new potatoes, apple, watercress and cucumber.

INGREDIENTS

125 g/4½ oz new potatoes, scrubbed and diced

225 g/8 oz mackerel fillets, skinned

1.2 litres/2 pints water

1 bay leaf

1 slice of lemon

1 eating apple, cored and diced

1 shallot, thinly sliced

3 tbsp white wine vinegar

1 tsp sunflower oil

1½ tsp caster sugar

¼ tsp Dijon mustard

salt and pepper

TO SERVE

2 tbsp low-fat natural yogurt

¼ cucumber, thinly sliced

1 tbsp snipped fresh chives

1 bunch of watercress

NUTRITIONAL INFORMATION

Calories	182
Protein	12g
Carbohydrate	11g
Sugars	6g
Fat	10g
Saturates	2g

variation

Fresh salmon is very versatile and would work equally well in this dish. Replace the mackerel fillets with the same quantity of salmon fillets.

cook's tip

If new potatoes such as Jersey Royals are not in season, use a waxy, firm-fleshed salad variety, such as Pink Fir Apple or Desirée.

1 Steam the potatoes over a saucepan of simmering water for 10 minutes, or until tender. Meanwhile, using a sharp knife, remove the skin from the mackerel fillets and cut into bite-sized pieces. Bring the water to the boil in a large, shallow saucepan, then reduce the heat so that it is just simmering and add the

mackerel pieces, bay leaf and lemon. Poach for 3 minutes, or until the flesh is opaque. Remove the mackerel from the saucepan with a spatula and transfer to a serving dish.

2 Drain the potatoes well and transfer them to a large bowl. Mix with the apple and shallot, then spoon the mixture over the mackerel.

3 Mix the vinegar, oil, sugar and mustard together in a jug, season to taste with salt and pepper and whisk thoroughly. Pour the dressing over the potato mixture. Cover and chill in the refrigerator for up to 6 hours.

4 To serve, spread the yogurt over the salad, then arrange the cucumber

decoratively on top and sprinkle with the fresh chives. Surround the salad with the watercress.

thai potato crab cakes

serves 4   **prep: 10 mins** ⏲   **cook: 30 mins** ⏲

These small crab cakes are based on a traditional Thai recipe. They make a delicious snack any time of the day when served with this sweet and sour cucumber sauce.

INGREDIENTS

450 g/1 lb floury potatoes, peeled and diced	**SAUCE**
	4 tbsp finely chopped cucumber
175 g/6 oz white crabmeat, drained if canned	2 tbsp clear honey
	1 tbsp garlic wine vinegar
4 spring onions, chopped	½ tsp light soy sauce
1 tsp light soy sauce	1 fresh red chilli, deseeded and chopped
½ tsp sesame oil	
1 tsp chopped lemon grass	
1 tsp lime juice	**TO GARNISH**
3 tbsp plain flour, plus extra for dusting	1 fresh red chilli, deseeded and sliced
salt and pepper	cucumber slices
2 tbsp vegetable oil	

NUTRITIONAL INFORMATION

Calories 254

Protein 12g

Carbohydrate 40g

Sugars 9g

Fat 6g

Saturates 1g

variation

If you like, replace the white crabmeat with canned tuna, drained and flaked, and the lime juice with lemon juice.

cook's tip

Fresh chillies can burn the skin several hours after chopping, so it is best to wear gloves when handling them. Alternatively, wash your hands thoroughly afterwards.

1 Cook the diced potatoes in a large saucepan of boiling water for 10 minutes, or until cooked through. Drain well and mash.

2 Mix the crabmeat into the mashed potato with the spring onions, soy sauce, sesame oil, lemon grass, lime juice and flour. Season to taste with salt and pepper.

3 Divide the potato mixture into 8 equal-sized portions and form them into small rounds, using floured hands. Heat the vegetable oil in a preheated wok or large, heavy-based frying pan and cook the cakes, 4 at a time, for 5–7 minutes, turning once. Transfer to a plate and keep warm. Repeat with the remaining crab cakes.

4 Meanwhile, make the sauce. Mix the cucumber, honey, vinegar, soy sauce and chopped red chilli together in a small bowl. Garnish the cakes with the sliced red chilli and cucumber slices and serve immediately with the sauce.

cantaloupe & crab salad

serves 4   **prep: 15 mins**   **cook: 0 mins**

This colourful salad combines delicious fresh crabmeat with flavoursome raw fruit and vegetables and a low-fat dressing – what could be healthier or more delicious?

INGREDIENTS

350 g/12 oz fresh crabmeat

5 tbsp Low-fat Mayonnaise (see page 12)

50 ml/2 fl oz low-fat natural yogurt

4 tsp extra virgin olive oil

4 tsp lime juice

1 spring onion, finely chopped

4 tsp finely chopped fresh parsley

pinch of cayenne pepper

1 cantaloupe melon

2 radicchio heads, separated into leaves

fresh parsley sprigs, to garnish

NUTRITIONAL INFORMATION

Calories	.252
Protein	.20g
Carbohydrate	.10g
Sugars	.9g
Fat	.15g
Saturates	.1g

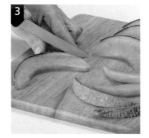

cook's tip

If fresh crabmeat is not available, you can use frozen crabmeat. Allow the crab to thaw thoroughly before making the salad.

1   Place the crabmeat in a large bowl and pick over it very carefully to remove any remaining shell or cartilage, but try not to break the meat up.

2   Place the Low-fat Mayonnaise, yogurt, olive oil, lime juice, spring onion, chopped fresh parsley and cayenne pepper into a separate bowl and mix until thoroughly blended. Fold in the crabmeat.

3   Cut the melon in half and remove and discard the seeds. Thinly slice, then cut off the rind with a sharp knife.

4   Arrange the melon slices and radicchio leaves on 4 large serving plates, then arrange the crabmeat mixture on top. Garnish with a few sprigs of fresh parsley and serve.

thai noodle salad

⏲ **cook: 3 mins**　　　⏲ **prep: 10 mins, plus 30 mins soaking**　　　**serves 4**

Thai salads are typically a contrasting mix of colours, textures, aromas and flavours, and are designed to delight the eye as much as they tempt the taste buds.

NUTRITIONAL INFORMATION	
Calories	.272
Protein	.16g
Carbohydrate	.45g
Sugars	.6g
Fat	.3g
Saturates	.1g

INGREDIENTS

25 g/1 oz dried wood ears

55 g/2 oz dried Chinese mushrooms

115 g/4 oz cellophane noodles

115 g/4 oz cooked lean minced pork

115 g/4 oz peeled raw prawns

5 fresh red chillies, deseeded and thinly sliced

1 tbsp chopped fresh coriander

3 tbsp Thai fish sauce (nam pla)

3 tbsp lime juice

1 tbsp brown sugar

variation

For extra flavour, use the strained soaking water from the mushrooms – not the wood ears – for cooking the prawns and the cooked minced pork.

1 Put the wood ears and Chinese mushrooms in separate bowls and pour over enough boiling water to cover. Leave to soak for 30 minutes. After 20 minutes, put the cellophane noodles in a separate bowl and pour over enough hot water to cover. Leave the noodles to soak for 10 minutes, or according to the packet instructions.

2 Drain the wood ears, rinse thoroughly and cut into small pieces. Drain the mushrooms, squeezing out as much liquid as possible. Cut off and discard the stalks and cut the caps in half. Pour just enough water into a saucepan to cover the base and bring to the boil. Add the pork, prawns, wood ears and mushrooms and simmer, stirring, for 3 minutes, or until cooked through. Drain well. Drain the noodles and cut them into short lengths with kitchen scissors.

3 Place the chillies, coriander, fish sauce, lime juice and brown sugar in a salad bowl and stir until the sugar has dissolved. Add the noodles and prawn and pork mixture, toss well and serve.

turkey & rice salad

serves 4

prep: 15 mins, plus **10 mins cooling**

cook: 45 mins

Rice salads are perfect at any time of year and are both economical and very easy to prepare. To enjoy the delicate flavour of this dish, serve it while it is still warm.

INGREDIENTS

1 litre/1¾ pints Chicken Stock (see page 11)

175 g/6 oz mixed long-grain and wild rice

2 tbsp sunflower or corn oil

225 g/8 oz skinless, boneless turkey breast, trimmed of all visible fat and cut into thin strips

225 g/8 oz mangetout

115 g/4 oz oyster mushrooms, torn into pieces

55 g/2 oz shelled pistachio nuts, finely chopped

2 tbsp chopped fresh coriander

1 tbsp snipped fresh garlic chives

salt and pepper

1 tbsp balsamic vinegar

fresh garlic chives, to garnish

NUTRITIONAL INFORMATION

Calories	.373
Protein	.22g
Carbohydrate	.40g
Sugars	.2g
Fat	.14g
Saturates	.1g

variation

This salad would also look spectacular made with red rice. Cook as in the main recipe or follow the packet instructions.

cook's tip

Before adding any of the ingredients to the preheated hot wok, swirl the sunflower oil gently and carefully so that it coats the sides as well as the base of the wok.

1 Reserve 3 tablespoons of the Chicken Stock and bring the remainder to the boil in a large saucepan. Add the rice and cook for 30 minutes, or until tender. Drain and leave to cool slightly.

2 Meanwhile, heat 1 tablespoon of the oil in a preheated wok or frying pan. Stir-fry the turkey over a medium heat for 3–4 minutes, or until cooked through. Using a slotted spoon, transfer the turkey to a dish. Add the mangetout and mushrooms to the wok and stir-fry for 1 minute. Add the reserved stock, bring to the boil, then reduce the heat, cover and simmer for 3–4 minutes. Transfer the vegetables to the dish and leave to cool slightly.

3 Thoroughly mix the rice, turkey, mangetout, mushrooms, nuts, coriander and garlic chives together, then season to taste with salt and pepper. Drizzle with the remaining sunflower oil and the vinegar and garnish with fresh garlic chives. Serve warm.

crêpes with curried crab

serves 4   **prep: 25 mins, plus 30 mins standing**   **cook: 25 mins**

Home-made crêpes are delicious – here, white crabmeat is lightly flavoured with curry spices and tossed in a low-fat dressing.

INGREDIENTS

115 g/4 oz buckwheat flour

1 large egg, beaten

300 ml/10 fl oz skimmed milk

125 g/4½ oz frozen spinach, thawed, well drained and chopped

2 tsp vegetable oil

FILLING

350 g/12 oz white crabmeat

1 tsp mild curry powder

1 tbsp mango chutney

1 tbsp Low-Fat Mayonnaise (see page 12)

2 tbsp low-fat natural yogurt

2 tbsp chopped fresh coriander

TO SERVE

green salad

lemon wedges

NUTRITIONAL INFORMATION	
Calories	.279
Protein	.25g
Carbohydrate	.31g
Sugars	.9g
Fat	.7g
Saturates	.1g

variation

If you like, try lean diced chicken in a light white sauce or peeled prawns instead of the crab.

cook's tip

If you don't have a crêpe pan, then a small non-stick frying pan would be suitable. Before adding the batter to the pan, stir or whisk it thoroughly to remove any lumps.

1 Sift the flour into a large bowl and remove and discard any husks that remain in the sieve. Make a well in the centre of the flour and add the beaten egg. Using a balloon whisk, gradually whisk in the milk, then blend in the chopped spinach. Transfer the mixture to a large jug and leave to stand for 30 minutes.

2 To make the filling, mix all the ingredients together, except the coriander, in a large bowl. Cover and chill until required.

3 Whisk the batter. Brush a small crêpe pan with vegetable oil, then heat until hot. Pour in enough batter to cover the base thinly and cook for 1–2 minutes, then turn over and cook for 1 minute, or until golden. Transfer to a plate. Repeat to make 8 crêpes, layering them on the plate with baking paper.

4 Stir the coriander into the crab mixture. Fold each crêpe into quarters. Open one fold and fill with the crab mixture. Serve warm, with a salad and lemon wedges.

prawn & rice salad

serves 4   **prep: 10 mins,** ⟳ **plus 10 mins cooling**   **cook: 35 mins** ⟳

This colourful tropical salad is simplicity itself to prepare and tastes simply wonderful. For a special treat, you could use tiger prawns rather than their smaller Atlantic or Mediterranean cousins.

INGREDIENTS

175 g/6 oz mixed long-grain
and wild rice
salt and pepper
350 g/12 oz cooked, peeled prawns
1 mango, peeled, stoned and diced
4 spring onions, sliced
25 g/1 oz flaked almonds
1 tbsp finely chopped fresh mint

DRESSING

1 tbsp extra virgin olive oil
2 tsp lime juice
1 garlic clove, crushed
1 tsp clear honey
salt and pepper

NUTRITIONAL INFORMATION

Calories 345

Protein 25g

Carbohydrate 43g

Sugars 8g

Fat 8g

Saturates 1g

variation

Substitute the same quantity of fresh or drained canned crabmeat for the prawns, if you like.

cook's tip

If using tiger prawns for this dish instead of the ordinary ones, buy already cooked and peeled prawns, which are available from most large supermarkets.

1 Cook the rice in a large saucepan of lightly salted boiling water for 35 minutes, or until tender. Drain and transfer to a large bowl, then add the prawns.

2 To make the dressing, mix all the ingredients together in a large jug,

seasoning to taste with the salt and pepper, and whisk well until thoroughly blended. Pour the dressing over the rice and prawn mixture and leave to cool.

3 Add the mango, spring onions, almonds and mint to the salad and season

to taste with pepper. Stir thoroughly and transfer to a large serving dish and serve.

spicy chickpea snack

serves 4 **prep: 5 mins** ⏲ **cook: 10 mins** ⏲

You can use dried chickpeas, soaked overnight and cooked until soft, for this popular Indian snack, but the canned variety is just as flavoursome and works equally well.

INGREDIENTS

400 g/14 oz canned chickpeas, drained
2 medium potatoes, peeled
1 medium onion
2 tbsp tamarind paste
6 tbsp water
1 tsp chilli powder
2 tsp sugar
salt and pepper

TO GARNISH

1 tomato, sliced
2 fresh green chillies, chopped
fresh coriander leaves

NUTRITIONAL INFORMATION	
Calories	190
Protein	9g
Carbohydrate	34g
Sugars	4g
Fat	3g
Saturates	0.3g

cook's tip

Chickpeas have a nutty flavour and slightly crunchy texture. Indian cooks also grind these to make a flour called gram or besan, which is used to make breads and to thicken sauces.

1 Place the chickpeas in a small bowl and reserve until required.

2 Using a sharp knife, cut the potatoes into dice and cook in a large saucepan of boiling water for 7–8 minutes, or until cooked through. Drain the potatoes, return to the saucepan and reserve until required.

3 Using a sharp knife, finely chop the onion. Reserve until required.

4 Mix the tamarind paste and water together in a small bowl. Add the chilli powder, sugar and 1 teaspoon salt and mix again. Pour the mixture over the chickpeas. Add the reserved onion and the diced potatoes, and stir to mix. Season to taste with salt and pepper. Transfer to a serving bowl and garnish with tomato slices, chillies and fresh coriander leaves.

potato & mushroom hash

⏲ cook: 25–30 mins   ⏱ prep: 10 mins   serves 4

This is an easy one-pan dish, which is ideal for a very quick snack and packed with colour and flavour. You can add any other type of vegetable you have at hand.

NUTRITIONAL INFORMATION	
Calories 378	
Protein 18g	
Carbohydrate 20g	
Sugars 14g	
Fat 26g	
Saturates 7g	

INGREDIENTS

675 g/1 lb 8 oz potatoes, peeled and cubed

1 tbsp olive oil

2 garlic cloves, crushed

1 green pepper, deseeded and cubed

1 yellow pepper, deseeded and cubed

3 tomatoes, diced

75 g/2¾ oz button mushrooms, halved

1 tbsp Worcestershire sauce

2 tbsp chopped fresh basil

salt and pepper

fresh basil leaves, to garnish

cook's tip

Most brands of Worcestershire sauce contains anchovies. If cooking for vegetarians, make sure you use a vegetarian variety or omit it altogether.

1 Cook the potatoes in a large saucepan of boiling water for 7–8 minutes, or until tender. Drain well, return to the saucepan and reserve until required.

2 Heat the olive oil in a large, heavy-based frying pan over a medium heat. Add the potatoes and cook for 8–10 minutes, stirring constantly, until the potatoes are browned. Add the garlic and peppers to the frying pan and cook for 2–3 minutes.

3 Stir in the tomatoes and mushrooms and cook, stirring constantly, for 5–6 minutes. Stir in the Worcestershire sauce and chopped basil, season to taste with salt and pepper, then transfer to a large serving dish. Garnish with a few fresh basil leaves and serve.

sweet potato & bean salad

serves 4   **prep: 10 mins** ⏱   **cook: 10 mins** ⏱

This piquant vegetarian salad is a meal in itself or can be served as an accompaniment to chicken or fish. Choose a mixture of colourful salad leaves with a range of sweet and bitter flavours.

INGREDIENTS

1 sweet potato

4 baby carrots, halved

4 tomatoes

4 celery sticks, chopped

225 g/8 oz canned borlotti beans, drained and rinsed

115 g/4 oz mixed salad leaves, such as frisée, rocket, radicchio and oakleaf lettuce

1 tbsp sultanas

4 spring onions, finely chopped

125 ml/4 fl oz Honey and Yogurt Dressing (see Cook's Tip, page 12)

NUTRITIONAL INFORMATION

Calories 143

Protein 6g

Carbohydrate 29g

Sugars 22g

Fat 1g

Saturates 1g

variation

Substitute your favourite beans for the borlotti beans – cannellini or flageolets would be equally good.

cook's tip

Cook the sweet potato in boiling water until it is just tender, otherwise it will absorb too much water and become unpleasantly soggy.

 1 Peel and dice the sweet potato. Bring a saucepan of water to the boil over a medium heat. Add the sweet potato and cook for 10 minutes, or until tender. Drain, transfer to a bowl and reserve until required.

2 Cook the carrots in a separate saucepan of boiling water for 1 minute.

Drain thoroughly and add to the sweet potato. Cut the tops off the tomatoes and scoop out the seeds. Chop the flesh and add to the bowl with the celery and beans. Mix well.

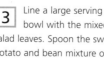 **3** Line a large serving bowl with the mixed salad leaves. Spoon the sweet potato and bean mixture on top, then sprinkle with the

sultanas and spring onions. Spoon over the dressing and serve immediately.

main dishes

*This chapter is the answer to that perennial question – what shall we have for
supper tonight? Finding a solution can be a real headache when every cookbook you turn to
for good ideas seems packed with recipes notable for their heavy use of butter, cream and other
high-fat ingredients. Inspired by cuisines around the world, from Greece to China and from
Morocco to Germany, these recipes feature marvellous main dishes based on meat,
poultry and vegetables. Many of them contain no more than 15 g (½ oz) fat per
serving and some contain far less.*

*Stun sceptical guests with Stuffed Pork Fillet (see page 124), Roast Turkey with
Cider Sauce (see page 150) or Moroccan Vegetable Stew (see page 154). No one will ever
suggest again that low-fat cooking is boring and bland. Seduce the family into a healthier
lifestyle with Swedish Lamb Stew (see page 138), Chicken with Saffron Mash (see page 140)
or Vegetable & Tofu Stir-fry (see page 152). Roasts, casseroles, stews, grills and stir-fries
are just some of the mouthwatering, healthy options that spoil you for choice. There is
a dish for every season and all tastes, from subtle and creamy to warm and spicy.
You will find quick and easy recipes for midweek suppers, succulent slow-cooked dishes
for restful weekends and gourmet delights for low-fat entertaining.*

beef & broccoli in black bean sauce

serves 4

prep: 10 mins,
plus 6 hrs marinating

cook: 15 mins

Stir-fries are not only quick and easy to cook, but a healthy choice as well. Because the cooking time is so brief, the vegetables retain most of their nutrients – and their flavour and texture too.

INGREDIENTS

225 g/8 oz lean rump steak

1 tbsp peanut or corn oil

225 g/8 oz broccoli, cut into florets

115 g/4 oz baby corn cobs,
cut in half diagonally

3 tbsp water

4 spring onions, sliced diagonally

225 g/8 oz canned water chestnuts,
drained, rinsed and sliced

MARINADE

1 tbsp fermented black beans, soaked
in cold water for 5–10 minutes

2 tbsp dark soy sauce

2 tbsp Chinese rice vinegar

1 tbsp peanut or corn oil

1 tsp brown sugar

1 garlic clove, thinly sliced

1 tbsp finely chopped fresh root ginger

NUTRITIONAL INFORMATION	
Calories	190
Protein	16g
Carbohydrate	12g
Sugars	3g
Fat	9g
Saturates	2g

variation

Use different combinations of vegetables for this stir-fry, such as courgette strips, carrot matchsticks, pepper strips and cucumber batons.

cook's tip

Fermented black beans are available in cans or bags from Chinese food shops. They should be soaked in cold water before use to remove any excess salt.

1 Using a sharp knife, trim the steak of all visible fat and thinly slice. Put the steak in a shallow, non-metallic dish. To make the marinade, mash the black beans in a bowl with a fork. Stir in the remaining ingredients until thoroughly blended. Pour the marinade over the steak, turning to coat thoroughly. Cover with clingfilm and leave in the refrigerator to marinate for up to 6 hours.

2 Heat the peanut oil in a preheated wok or large frying pan. Drain the steak and reserve the marinade. Stir-fry the steak over a medium–high heat for 3 minutes, then transfer to a plate. Add the broccoli and baby corn cobs to the wok and stir in the water. Cover and steam over a low heat for 5 minutes, or until the vegetables are tender.

3 Add the spring onions and water chestnuts to the wok. Stir-fry for 2 minutes. Return the steak to the wok and pour in the reserved marinade. Cook, stirring, until heated through, then serve.

meatballs with tomato relish

serves 4 **prep: 15 mins** **cook: 15–20 mins**

Even when minced beef is labelled 'lean', it may contain more fat than we would like. It is best to buy a whole piece of lean beef, such as rump steak, trim off all visible fat and mince it yourself.

INGREDIENTS

1 onion, finely chopped

2 garlic cloves, finely chopped

2 slices bread, crusts removed

500 g/1 lb 2 oz lean beef, minced

1 cooked baby beetroot, chopped

pinch of paprika

2 tsp finely chopped fresh thyme

1 egg

salt and pepper

fresh thyme sprigs, to garnish

TOMATO RELISH

150 ml/5 fl oz passata

2 tsp creamed horseradish

NUTRITIONAL INFORMATION	
Calories	243
Protein	30g
Carbohydrate	14g
Sugars	5g
Fat	8g
Saturates	3g

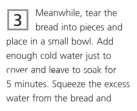

cook's tip

It is easy to cook beetroot yourself. Clean them and trim the stalks, then cook in a saucepan of simmering lightly salted water for 1–2 hours, or until tender. Drain and cool, then peel.

1 Preheat the oven to 230°C/450°F/Gas Mark 8. To make the tomato relish, mix the passata and creamed horseradish together in a small bowl. Cover and reserve until required.

2 Place the onion, garlic and 2 teaspoons of water in a small saucepan and simmer over a low heat for 5 minutes. Increase the heat, bring to the boil and cook until all the water has evaporated. Remove from the heat.

3 Meanwhile, tear the bread into pieces and place in a small bowl. Add enough cold water just to cover and leave to soak for 5 minutes. Squeeze the excess water from the bread and place in a bowl with the minced beef, onion and garlic mixture, beetroot, paprika, thyme and egg. Season to taste with salt and pepper and mix thoroughly.

4 Form the mixture into 24 small balls between the palms of your hands. Thread 3 balls on to each of 8 skewers and place on a baking sheet. Bake in the preheated oven for 10 minutes, or until well browned. Transfer to a serving dish, garnish with a few sprigs of fresh thyme and serve with the tomato relish.

beef in beer

⏱ **cook: 2 hrs–2 hrs 30 mins**   ◔ **prep: 15 mins**   **serves 4**

Beef and beer is a traditional combination in all brewing countries, especially in Belgium, Germany and Ireland. Use a strong dark beer or stout to create the fullest flavour.

NUTRITIONAL INFORMATION	
Calories	224
Protein	27g
Carbohydrate	6g
Sugars	5g
Fat	9g
Saturates	3g

INGREDIENTS

few sprigs of fresh parsley

1 tbsp sunflower or corn oil

500 g/1 lb 2 oz lean stewing steak, trimmed of all visible fat and cut into 2.5-cm/1-inch cubes

1 onion, chopped

200 g/7 oz chestnut mushrooms, cut in half

4 tsp dark muscovado sugar

350 ml/12 fl oz Beef Stock (see page 11)

300 ml/10 fl oz dark beer or stout

salt and pepper

variation

You could add 1 thinly sliced carrot and 2 thinly sliced celery sticks halfway through cooking the mushrooms in Step 2.

1 Using a sharp knife, chop the fresh parsley finely and reserve until required. Heat the sunflower oil in a large, heavy-based frying pan. Add the stewing steak and cook, stirring frequently, for 10 minutes, or until browned all over. Using a slotted spoon, transfer the meat to a large flameproof casserole dish.

2 Add the onion to the frying pan and cook over a low heat, stirring occasionally, for 3 minutes. Add the mushrooms and sugar and cook, stirring occasionally, for 10 minutes. Transfer to the casserole with a slotted spoon.

3 Add the beef stock, beer and reserved parsley to the casserole and season to taste with salt and pepper. Bring to the boil, cover and simmer over a very low heat for 1½–2 hours, or until tender. Serve hot.

chilli con carne

serves 4　　　　**prep: 5 mins** 🕑　　　　**cook: 2 hrs 30 mins** 🕒

Probably the most popular Mexican dish and one that is a great favourite with everyone. The chilli content can be increased to suit your taste. Serve with freshly cooked rice and tortillas, if you like.

INGREDIENTS

750 g/1 lb 10 oz lean braising
or stewing steak

2 tbsp vegetable oil

1 large onion, sliced

2–4 garlic cloves, crushed

1 tbsp plain flour

425 ml/15 fl oz tomato juice

400 g/14 oz canned tomatoes

1–2 tbsp sweet chilli sauce

1 tsp ground cumin

salt and pepper

425 g/15 oz canned red kidney beans,
drained and rinsed

½ teaspoon dried oregano

1–2 tbsp chopped fresh parsley

chopped fresh herbs, to garnish

TO SERVE

freshly cooked rice

tortillas

NUTRITIONAL INFORMATION
Calories 443
Protein 48g
Carbohydrate 30g
Sugars 11g
Fat 15g
Saturates 4g

variation

For a vegetarian version, replace the beef with 150 g/5½ oz mycoprotein (Quorn™) or cooked brown lentils and adjust the cooking time.

cook's tip

Because chilli con carne requires quite a lengthy cooking time, it saves time and fuel to prepare double the quantity you need and freeze half of it for another occasion. Thaw and use within 3–4 weeks.

1 Preheat the oven to 160°C/325°F/Gas Mark 3. Using a sharp knife, cut the beef into 2-cm/¾-inch cubes. Heat the vegetable oil in a large flameproof casserole dish and fry the beef over a medium heat until well sealed on all sides. Remove the beef from the casserole with a slotted spoon and reserve until required.

2 Add the onion and garlic to the casserole and fry until lightly browned; then stir in the flour and cook for 1–2 minutes.

3 Stir in the tomato juice and tomatoes and bring to the boil. Return the beef to the casserole and add the chilli sauce, cumin and salt and pepper to taste. Cover and

cook in the preheated oven for 1½ hours, or until the beef is almost tender.

4 Stir in the kidney beans, oregano and parsley, and adjust the seasoning to taste, if necessary. Cover the casserole and return to the oven for 45 minutes. Transfer to 4 large, warmed serving plates, sprinkle with chopped

fresh herbs and serve immediately with freshly cooked rice and tortillas.

rogan josh

⏲ cook: 1 hr 45 mins   **◷ prep: 10 mins**   **serves 6**

NUTRITIONAL INFORMATION	
Calories	.248
Protein	.35g
Carbohydrate	.2g
Sugars	.2g
Fat	.11g
Saturates	.5g

variation

Replace the ghee with vegetable oil and if you like the dish less spicy, deseed the chillies before using.

This is one of the best-known curries. Rogan Josh means 'red curry', and is so-called because of the red chillies in the recipe.

INGREDIENTS

2 tbsp ghee	2 tsp coriander seeds
1 kg/2 lb 4 oz lean braising steak, cut into 2.5-cm/1-inch cubes	2 tsp cumin seeds
1 onion, chopped finely	1 tsp paprika
3 garlic cloves	1 tsp salt
2.5-cm/1-inch piece fresh root ginger, grated	1 bay leaf
4 fresh red chillies, chopped	125 ml/4 fl oz low-fat natural yogurt
4 green cardamom pods	2.5-cm/1-inch piece cinnamon stick
4 cloves	150 ml/5 fl oz hot water
	pepper
	¼ tsp garam masala

cook's tip

Use a spice mill, coffee grinder or the more traditional pestle and mortar to grind spices. If using a coffee grinder, wash it thoroughly afterwards.

 1 Preheat the oven to 180°C/350°F/Gas Mark 4. Heat the ghee in a large flameproof casserole and brown the steak in batches. Remove the steak from the casserole and place in a bowl. Reserve until required.

 2 Add the chopped onion to the casserole and cook for 3–4 minutes.

3 Place the garlic, ginger, chillies, cardamoms, cloves, coriander, cumin, paprika and salt in a mortar, and using a pestle, grind to a paste. Add the spice paste and bay leaf to the casserole and stir until fragrant.

4 Return the meat and any juices in the bowl to the casserole and simmer for 2–3 minutes. Gradually stir in the yogurt, keeping the sauce simmering. Add the cinnamon stick and stir in the water. Add pepper to taste.

5 Cover the casserole and cook in the preheated oven for 1¼ hours, or until the meat is very tender and the sauce is slightly reduced. Remove and discard the cinnamon stick and stir in the garam masala. Remove surplus oil from the surface of the casserole before serving.

sauerbraten

serves 4

prep: 20 mins, plus 48 hrs marinating

cook: 2 hrs 15 mins

In this traditional German dish, long marinating makes the topside melt-in-the-mouth tender and imparts a marvellous spicy flavour. This dish makes the perfect treat for a special occasion.

INGREDIENTS

750 g/1 lb 10 oz topside of beef, trimmed of all visible fat

8 whole cloves

1 tbsp sunflower or corn oil

225 ml/8 fl oz Beef Stock (see page 11)

1 kg/2 lb 4 oz mixed root vegetables, such as carrots, potatoes and swede, peeled and cut into large chunks

2 tbsp raisins

1½ tsp cornflour

3 tbsp water

salt and pepper

MARINADE

200 ml/7 fl oz wine

5 tbsp red wine vinegar

1 onion, chopped

1½ tsp brown sugar

4 peppercorns

1 bay leaf

½ tsp ground mixed spice

½ tsp mustard

NUTRITIONAL INFORMATION	
Calories	.445
Protein	.41g
Carbohydrate	.36g
Sugars	.25g
Fat	.12g
Saturates	.4g

variation

Try other root vegetables with this dish, such as chunks of parsnip, turnip and celeriac.

cook's tip

This rustic dish will taste superb if you serve it with a simple and traditional accompaniment of boiled potatoes or noodles.

1 To make the marinade, place all the ingredients, except the mustard, in a saucepan. Bring to simmering point, then remove from the heat and stir in the mustard. Stud the beef with cloves and place in a non-metallic dish. Pour the marinade over, cover and leave to cool, then chill in the refrigerator for 2 days. About 1 hour before cooking,

remove the beef, pat dry and stand at room temperature. Reserve the marinade.

2 Preheat the oven to 150°C/300°F/Gas Mark 2. Heat the oil in a flameproof casserole, add the beef and cook over a medium heat for 5–10 minutes, or until browned. Pour the marinade into the casserole through a

sieve, add the stock and bring to the boil. Cover and bake in the oven for 1 hour, turning and basting frequently with the cooking juices.

3 Meanwhile, blanch the vegetables in boiling water for 3 minutes, then drain. Arrange the vegetables around the beef, return to the oven and cook for 1 hour, or

until the beef is very tender and the vegetables are cooked.

4 Transfer the beef and vegetables to a serving dish. Place the casserole on a low heat and add the raisins. Mix the cornflour and water until smooth and stir into the cooking juices. Bring to the boil, stirring, then simmer for 2–3 minutes. Season and serve.

stuffed pork fillet

serves 8   prep: 25 mins, plus 6 hrs chilling (optional)   cook: 1 hr 30 mins

Dried fruit, such as prunes and apricots, balances the richness of pork superbly. This succulent pork fillet is perfect served hot for a family supper and would also be an excellent choice, served cold, for a buffet, summer party or picnic.

INGREDIENTS

2 pork fillets, about 500 g/1 lb 2 oz each, trimmed of all visible fat

STUFFING

2 red onions, finely chopped

115 g/4 oz fresh wholemeal breadcrumbs

85 g/3 oz no-soak dried prunes, chopped

85 g/3 oz no-soak dried apricots, chopped

pinch of grated nutmeg

pinch of ground cinnamon

salt and pepper

1 egg white, lightly beaten

NUTRITIONAL INFORMATION	
Calories	265
Protein	29g
Carbohydrate	17g
Sugars	11g
Fat	9g
Saturates	3g

variation

For an elegant presentation, garnish the pork fillet with fresh watercress and serve, adding a few watercress leaves to each plate.

cook's tip

Dried fruit that does not need soaking is often labelled as 'ready-to-eat' fruit, and is available in the baking section of most large supermarkets.

1 Preheat the oven to 200°C/400°F/Gas Mark 6. To make the stuffing, mix the onions, breadcrumbs, prunes and apricots together. Season to taste with nutmeg, cinnamon, and salt and pepper. Stir in the egg white.

2 Cut a 13-cm/5-inch long piece from the narrow end of each pork fillet, then cut all the pieces almost completely in half lengthways and open them out. Spread half the filling evenly over one of the longer pieces, then cover with both the smaller pieces, overlapping the narrow ends slightly. Spread the remaining filling on top and cover with the remaining piece of pork. Tie the pork loaf together with kitchen string or trussing thread at intervals along its length. Wrap it securely in foil and place in a roasting tin.

3 Cook the pork in the preheated oven for 1½ hours. If serving hot, leave to stand for 10 minutes before unwrapping, cutting off the string and slicing. If serving cold, leave to cool in the wrapping, then leave to chill in the refrigerator for at least 2 hours and up to 6 hours before unwrapping and slicing.

stir-fried pork with mangetout

serves 4 **prep: 25 mins, plus** ⏲ **40 mins standing/chilling** **cook: 20 mins** ⏲

Served with rice or noodles, this substantial stir-fry makes a delicious midweek family supper. Prepare the garnish before you begin cooking and serve with a flourish.

INGREDIENTS

8 dried Chinese mushrooms

450 g/1 lb pork fillet, trimmed of all visible fat and cut into thin strips

115 g/4 oz baby corn cobs

1 tbsp groundnut or corn oil

1 garlic clove, finely chopped

2.5-cm/1-inch piece fresh root ginger, cut into thin batons

400 g/14 oz mangetout

400 g/14 oz canned bamboo shoots, drained, rinsed and thinly sliced

2 tsp dark soy sauce

2 tsp Chinese rice wine

4 tbsp Chicken or Vegetable Stock (see page 11)

2 tsp cornflour

2 tbsp water

1 carrot, sliced into thin batons

salt and pepper

1–2 spring onions, trimmed, to garnish

MARINADE

1 tbsp dark soy sauce

1 tbsp Chinese rice wine

2 tsp cornflour

pepper

NUTRITIONAL INFORMATION	
Calories	309
Protein	31g
Carbohydrate	22g
Sugars	5g
Fat	12g
Saturates	3g

variation

You could add an extra, thinly sliced carrot and 2 thinly sliced celery sticks halfway through cooking the mushrooms in Step 4, if you like.

cook's tip

To rehydrate dried Chinese mushrooms, place the mushrooms in a small bowl and pour over enough hot water to cover. Leave to soak for 20 minutes.

 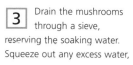

1 To make the garnish, make a lengthways cut 2.5-cm/1-inch long at one end of each spring onion. Roll the onion through 90° and repeat. Repeat at the other end, then place in iced water to open out. Pat dry before using.

2 Rehydrate the Chinese mushrooms (see Cook's Tip). Mix all the marinade ingredients together in a non-metallic dish, seasoning with the pepper. Add the pork, cover and chill for 20 minutes. Blanch the corn in boiling water for 5 minutes. Drain and refresh in cold water.

3 Drain the mushrooms through a sieve, reserving the soaking water. Squeeze out any excess water, remove the stems and slice the caps. Heat half the oil in a preheated wok, add the pork and stir-fry for 5 minutes, until browned. Remove and reserve.

4 Wipe the wok, add the remaining oil and heat. Add the garlic and cook until golden. Remove with a slotted spoon and discard. Add the ginger, mangetout, bamboo shoots and mushrooms and stir-fry for 3 minutes. Stir in the soy sauce, wine, stock and reserved soaking liquid. Cook for 2–3 minutes. Mix the cornflour and water, add to the wok and stir until thickened. Return the pork and cooking juices to the wok, add the corn and cook until heated through. Stir in the carrot, garnish with spring onion tassels and serve.

char shiu pork

serves 4

prep: 20 mins, plus 2 hrs marinating

cook: 15–20 mins

The aromatic star anise gives this very famous traditional Cantonese dish its characteristic flavour, while the dark soy sauce is the secret of the rich and appetizing colour.

INGREDIENTS

600 g/1 lb 5 oz pork fillet, trimmed of all visible fat

2 tbsp dark soy sauce

2 spring onions, finely chopped

2.5-cm/1-inch piece fresh root ginger, finely chopped

1 tsp red fermented bean curd

2 star anise

1 tbsp Chinese rice wine

1 tbsp clear honey

1½ tsp Chinese rice vinegar

½ tsp cornflour

1 tbsp water

NUTRITIONAL INFORMATION

Calories 260

Protein 32g

Carbohydrate 9g

Sugars 5g

Fat 11g

Saturates 4g

cook's tip

Char shui pork can also be cooked on a preheated barbecue. Cook for 15 minutes over hot coals, turning and brushing frequently with the glaze.

1 Brush the pork all over with half the soy sauce and leave to stand for 15 minutes. Meanwhile, place the spring onions, ginger, bean curd and star anise in a mortar and pound to a paste with a pestle. Transfer to a shallow, non-metallic dish and stir in the Chinese rice wine, half the honey, 1 teaspoon of the vinegar and the remaining soy sauce. Add the pork, turning to coat. Cover and leave in the refrigerator to marinate for 2 hours, turning the pork every 20 minutes.

2 Preheat the oven to 220°C/425°F/Gas Mark 7. Remove the pork from the marinade and pat dry with kitchen paper. Reserve the marinade. Mix the remaining honey and vinegar with 1 teaspoon of hot water in a small bowl and brush the glaze all over the pork. Place the pork on a rack in a roasting tin and roast in the oven for 10–12 minutes, or until the juices run clear when the meat is pierced with a skewer. Turn the pork once during cooking and brush with the remaining honey glaze.

3 Remove the pork from the oven, cover with foil and leave to stand for 10 minutes. Meanwhile, bring the reserved marinade to the boil in a saucepan. Mix the cornflour and water until smooth, add to the marinade and stir until thickened. Cut the pork across the grain into 5-mm/¼ inch slices. Serve with the marinade for dipping.

griddled pork with orange sauce

🕐 **cook: 10 mins**

🕐 **prep: 10 mins, plus 3 hrs marinating**

serves 4

In this recipe, the pork is garnished with gremolata, a popular Italian seasoning mixture with a citrus tang, which gives the dish a refreshing summery flavour.

NUTRITIONAL INFORMATION

Calories	204
Protein	26g
Carbohydrate	2g
Sugars	1g
Fat	10g
Saturates	3g

INGREDIENTS

4 tbsp freshly squeezed orange juice

4 tbsp red wine vinegar

2 garlic cloves, finely chopped

pepper

4 pork steaks, trimmed of all visible fat

olive oil, for brushing

GREMOLATA

3 tbsp finely chopped fresh parsley

grated rind of 1 lime

grated rind of ½ lemon

1 garlic clove, very finely chopped

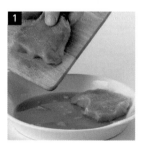

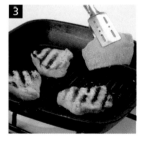

variation

This dish would work equally well with chicken breast portions. Remove the skin from the cooked chicken before serving.

1 Mix the orange juice, vinegar and garlic together in a shallow, non-metallic dish and season to taste with pepper. Add the pork, turning to coat. Cover and leave in the refrigerator to marinate for up to 3 hours.

2 Meanwhile, mix all the gremolata ingredients together in a small mixing bowl, cover with clingfilm and leave to chill in the refrigerator until required.

3 Heat a non-stick griddle pan and brush lightly with olive oil. Remove the pork from the marinade, reserving the marinade, add to the pan and cook over a medium–high heat for 5 minutes on each side, or until the juices run clear when the meat is pierced with a skewer.

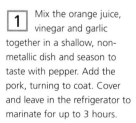

4 Meanwhile, pour the marinade into a small saucepan and simmer over a medium heat for 5 minutes, or until slightly thickened. Transfer the pork to a serving dish, pour the orange sauce over it and sprinkle with the gremolata. Serve immediately.

pork with fennel & aniseed

serves 4   **prep: 20 mins**   **cook: 35 mins**

Lean pork chops, stuffed with an aniseed and orange filling, are pan-cooked with fennel in an aniseed-flavoured sweet sauce.

INGREDIENTS

4 lean pork chops, about
125 g/4½ oz each

55 g/2 oz brown rice, cooked

1 tsp orange rind, grated

4 spring onions, trimmed
and finely chopped

salt and pepper

½ tsp aniseed

1 tbsp olive oil

1 fennel bulb, trimmed
and thinly sliced

450 ml/16 fl oz unsweetened
orange juice

1 tbsp cornflour

2 tbsp Pernod

fennel fronds, to garnish

cooked vegetables, to serve

NUTRITIONAL INFORMATION	
Calories	.298
Protein	.30g
Carbohydrate	.18g
Sugars	.10g
Fat	.10g
Saturates	.3g

variation

If you find the aniseed flavour slightly too intense, then omit the Pernod and blend the cornflour with 2 tablespoons of water instead.

cook's tip

To prepare fennel, rinse under cold running water. Using a sharp knife, cut off the base and the tops, reserving the feathery fronds for garnish. Remove the tough outer leaves and slice lengthways.

1 Using a sharp knife, trim away any excess fat from the pork chops and make a slit in the centre of each chop to create a pocket.

2 Mix the rice, orange rind, spring onions, salt and pepper and aniseed together in a bowl. Push the rice mixture into the pocket of each chop, then press to seal.

3 Heat the olive oil in a frying pan and fry the pork chops on each side for 2–3 minutes, or until lightly browned. Add the fennel and orange juice to the frying pan, bring to the boil and simmer for 15–20 minutes, or until the meat is tender and cooked through. Remove the pork and fennel with a slotted spoon and transfer to a serving plate.

4 Blend the cornflour and Pernod together in a small bowl. Add the cornflour mixture to the frying pan and stir into the pan juices. Cook for 2–3 minutes, stirring, until the sauce thickens. Pour the Pernod sauce over the pork chops, garnish with fennel fronds and serve immediately with freshly cooked vegetables.

pork with plums

serves 4

prep: 15 mins, plus ⏲ **30 mins marinating**

cook: 25 mins ⏲

Plum sauce is often used in Chinese cooking with pork, duck or other rich meat to counteract the flavour.

INGREDIENTS

450 g/1 lb pork fillet

1 tbsp cornflour

2 tbsp light soy sauce

2 tbsp Chinese rice wine

4 tsp light brown sugar

pinch of ground cinnamon

5 tsp vegetable oil

2 garlic cloves, crushed

2 spring onions, chopped

4 tbsp plum sauce

1 tbsp hoisin sauce

150 ml/5 fl oz water

dash of chilli sauce

fried plum quarters (see Cook's Tip)

spring onions slices, to garnish

NUTRITIONAL INFORMATION

Calories	281
Protein	. . . . .25g
Carbohydrate	. . . . .10g
Sugars	. . . . .6g
Fat	. . . . .11g
Saturates	. . . . .4g

cook's tip

For the garnish, cut 2 ripe plums into quarters. Heat 2 teaspoons of oil in a hot wok or frying pan and add the plums. Stir-fry for a few minutes, then remove and drain on kitchen paper.

1 Cut the pork fillet into thin slices. Mix the cornflour, soy sauce, Chinese rice wine, sugar and cinnamon together in a small bowl.

2 Place the pork in a shallow, non-metallic dish and pour the cornflour mixture over it. Toss the meat in the marinade until it is completely coated. Cover with

clingfilm and leave to marinate in the refrigerator for at least 30 minutes.

3 Using a slotted spoon, remove the pork from the dish, reserving the marinade. Heat the vegetable oil in a preheated wok or large frying pan. Add the pork and stir-fry for 3–4 minutes, or until a light golden colour.

4 Stir in the garlic, spring onions, plum sauce, hoisin sauce, water and chilli sauce and bring to the boil. Reduce the heat, cover and simmer for 8–10 minutes, or until the pork is cooked through and tender.

5 Stir in the reserved marinade and cook, stirring, for 5 minutes.

6 Transfer the pork stir-fry to a warmed serving dish and garnish with fried plum quarters and spring onion slices. Serve immediately.

pork stroganoff

🍳 **cook: 30 mins**   ⏲ **prep: 20 mins**   **serves 4**

Tender, lean pork, cooked in a delicious rich tomato sauce is flavoured with the extra tang of natural yogurt.

NUTRITIONAL INFORMATION

Calories 223	
Protein 22g	
Carbohydrate 12g	
Sugars 7g	
Fat 10g	
Saturates 3g	

INGREDIENTS

350 g/12 oz lean pork fillet

1 tbsp vegetable oil

1 medium onion, chopped

2 garlic cloves, crushed

25 g/1 oz plain flour

2 tbsp tomato purée

425 ml/15 fl oz Chicken or Vegetable
Stock (see page 11)

125 g/4½ oz button mushrooms, sliced

1 large green pepper, deseeded

salt and pepper

½ tsp freshly grated nutmeg, plus extra
to garnish

4 tbsp low-fat natural yogurt

boiled rice with chopped fresh parsley,
to serve

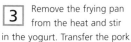

cook's tip

You can buy ready-made stock from leading supermarkets. Although more expensive, this is more nutritious than stock cubes, which are high in salt and artificial flavourings.

1 Trim away any excess fat and silver skin from the pork, then cut the meat into 1-cm/½-inch thick slices. Heat the vegetable oil in a large, heavy-based frying pan and gently fry the pork, onion and garlic for 4–5 minutes, or until lightly browned.

2 Stir in the flour and tomato purée, then pour in the Chicken Stock and stir to mix thoroughly. Add the mushrooms, pepper, salt and pepper to taste and nutmeg. Bring to the boil, cover and simmer for 20 minutes, or until the pork is tender and cooked through.

3 Remove the frying pan from the heat and stir in the yogurt. Transfer the pork to 4 large, warmed serving plates and serve with boiled rice sprinkled with chopped fresh parsley and an extra spoonful of yogurt, garnished with freshly grated nutmeg.

lamb tagine

serves 4   **prep: 10 mins**   **cook: 1 hr 40 mins**

This is a typical Moroccan mixture of meat, vegetables and apricots, flavoured with plenty of fresh herbs and spices. It is delicious – and authentic – if served with couscous, which can be cooked in a steamer set over the stew for 6–7 minutes.

INGREDIENTS

1 tbsp sunflower or corn oil	1 cinnamon stick
1 onion, chopped	1-cm/½-inch piece fresh root ginger,
350 g/12 oz boneless lamb,	finely chopped
trimmed of all visible fat and	1 aubergine
cut into 2.5-cm/1-inch cubes	4 tomatoes, peeled and chopped
1 garlic clove, finely chopped	115 g/4 oz no-soak dried apricots
600 ml/1 pint Vegetable Stock	2 tbsp chopped fresh coriander
(see page 11)	salt and pepper
grated rind and juice of 1 orange	freshly cooked couscous, to serve
1 tsp clear honey	

NUTRITIONAL INFORMATION

Calories 267

Protein 21g

Carbohydrate 22g

Sugars 21g

Fat 11g

Saturates 4g

variation

This stew can also be made with the same quantity of no-soak prunes. Alternatively, add 55 g/2 oz no-soak apricots and 55 g/2 oz raisins.

cook's tip

Large aubergines benefit from being sprinkled with salt and left to stand for 30 minutes to remove the bitter juices. Smaller aubergines can be used without salting.

1 Heat the sunflower oil in a large, heavy-based frying pan or flameproof casserole. Add the onion and lamb cubes and cook over a medium heat, stirring frequently, for 5 minutes, or until the meat is lightly browned all over. Add the garlic, Vegetable Stock, orange rind and juice, honey, cinnamon stick and ginger.

2 Using a sharp knife, halve the aubergine lengthways and slice thinly. Add to the frying pan with the chopped tomatoes and apricots. Cover and cook for a further 45 minutes, or until the lamb is tender.

Bring to the boil, then reduce the heat, cover and simmer for 45 minutes.

3 Stir in the coriander, season to taste with salt and pepper and serve immediately, straight from the frying pan, with the freshly cooked couscous.

greek lamb parcel

serves 4   **prep: 25 mins, plus 8 hrs marinating**   **cook: 35 mins**

Steaming is an excellent low-fat cooking technique. It is essential that the steamer has a tight-fitting lid. If it doesn't, wrap a clean tea towel around the lid to ensure it fits snugly.

INGREDIENTS

500 g/1 lb 2 oz boneless lamb, trimmed of all visible fat and cut into small cubes
2 tsp olive oil
1 red pepper, deseeded and finely chopped
4 tomatoes, peeled and roughly chopped
1 aubergine, roughly chopped
1 courgette, roughly chopped
4 shallots, cut into wedges
salt and pepper
1 tbsp chopped fresh mint

1 tbsp snipped fresh chives
100 ml/3½ fl oz Vegetable Stock (see page 11)
150 ml/5 fl oz low-fat natural yogurt
fresh rosemary sprigs, to garnish

MARINADE
4 tsp mavrodaphne or sweet sherry
1 shallot, finely chopped
1 garlic clove, finely chopped
1 tsp olive oil
salt and pepper

NUTRITIONAL INFORMATION	
Calories	.310
Protein	.30g
Carbohydrate	.12g
Sugars	.11g
Fat	.14g
Saturates	.6g

variation

Boneless leg of lamb is also ideal for this dish. If shallots are unavailable, replace with 1 sliced onion.

cook's tip

During the marinating process, turn the meat occasionally with a slotted spoon. Before cooking, drain the meat thoroughly and bring it to room temperature.

1 Place the lamb in a non-metallic dish. Mix all the marinade ingredients together in a bowl, seasoning to taste. Pour the marinade over the lamb, turning to coat well. Cover and leave in the refrigerator to marinate for 8 hours, or overnight. Remove the lamb from the marinade and pat dry with kitchen paper. Reserve the marinade.

2 Heat the olive oil in a large, heavy-based frying pan. Add the lamb and cook, stirring, for 5 minutes, or until browned. Stir in the pepper, tomatoes, aubergine, courgette and shallots and season to taste. Cut a piece of foil large enough to contain the lamb mixture and spoon the mixture on to it, sprinkle with half the mint and half the chives and turn up the edges of the foil. Return the pan to the heat, add the stock and bring to the boil, scraping up any sediment on the base. Boil until thickened, then pour over the lamb. Seal the foil parcel and place in a steamer set over a saucepan of boiling water. Cover and steam for 30 minutes, topping up with more water, if necessary.

3 Meanwhile, bring the marinade to the boil in a saucepan. Stir in the remaining mint and chives, then remove from the heat and leave to cool. Transfer the lamb mixture to a warmed dish. Stir the yogurt into the marinade and pour over the lamb. Garnish with rosemary sprigs and serve.

swedish lamb stew

serves 4   **prep: 15 mins** ⟲   **cook: 2 hrs** ⟳

This hearty, dill-flavoured lamb stew is a welcome sight on a cold winter evening. Serve with steamed vegetables and plenty of crusty bread to mop up the delicious juices, if you like.

INGREDIENTS

450 g/1 lb boneless lamb	115 g/4 oz puffball mushrooms
salt and white pepper	2 tsp cornflour
1 onion, cut into wedges	1 tbsp skimmed milk
2 fresh dill sprigs	grated rind and juice of ½ lemon
1 bay leaf	150 ml/5 fl oz Greek-style yogurt
6 green peppercorns	1 tsp mild mustard
1 fennel bulb, thinly sliced	4 tbsp snipped fresh dill

NUTRITIONAL INFORMATION

Calories	.276
Protein	.28g
Carbohydrate	.11g
Sugars	.5g
Fat	.14g
Saturates	.7g

variation

If you prefer, you can substitute whole button mushrooms for the puffball mushrooms.

cook's tip

If you have more cooking liquid than you require in Step 2, cool and freeze the excess to use in another lamb dish. As lamb stock is strongly flavoured, do not use it with other types of meat or poultry.

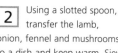 **1** Using a sharp knife, trim off all visible fat from the lamb and cut into 2.5-cm/1-inch cubes. Place the lamb in a large saucepan and cover with cold water. Add a pinch of salt. Bring to the boil over a medium heat and, using a slotted spoon, skim off any scum that rises to the surface. Add the onion, dill sprigs, bay leaf and peppercorns. Reduce the heat, cover and simmer for 45 minutes. Add the fennel and mushrooms, cover and simmer for 30 minutes, or until the lamb is very tender.

2 Using a slotted spoon, transfer the lamb, onion, fennel and mushrooms to a dish and keep warm. Sieve the cooking liquid and reserve 300 ml/10 fl oz. Rinse the pan, pour in the reserved cooking liquid and bring to the boil. Mix the cornflour and milk until smooth and stir into the sauce. Reduce the heat and simmer, stirring, for 5 minutes, or until thickened. Stir in the lemon rind and juice.

 3 Return the lamb, onion, fennel and mushrooms to the saucepan and simmer, uncovered, for 5 minutes. Meanwhile, mix the yogurt, mustard and snipped dill together in a small bowl and season to taste with salt and pepper. Stir the yogurt mixture into the stew, transfer to a warmed serving dish and serve immediately.

chicken with saffron mash

serves 4　　　　**prep: 20 mins**　　　　**cook: 25 mins**

The addition of fresh thyme, coriander and lemon juice complements the griddled chicken and saffron mash to perfection. Serve with freshly cooked steamed vegetables, such as carrots, broccoli and French beans, if you like.

INGREDIENTS

550 g/1 lb 4 oz floury potatoes, cut into chunks	2 tbsp olive oil
1 garlic clove, peeled	1 tbsp lemon juice
1 tsp saffron threads, crushed	1 tbsp chopped fresh thyme
1.2 litres/2 pints Chicken or Vegetable Stock (see page 11)	1 tbsp chopped fresh coriander
4 skinless, boneless chicken breasts, trimmed of all visible fat	1 tbsp coriander seeds, crushed
	100 ml/3½ fl oz hot skimmed milk
	salt and pepper
	fresh thyme sprigs, to garnish

NUTRITIONAL INFORMATION

Calories	310
Protein	. . . . .31g
Carbohydrate	. . . . .25g
Sugars	. . . . .2g
Fat	. . . . .10g
Saturates	. . . . .2g

variation

Serve sweet potato cream instead. Bake 550 g/1 lb 4 oz sweet potatoes for 1 hour. Scoop out the flesh and mash. Heat and stir in a little butter.

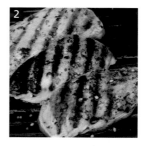

cook's tip

Reserve the stock when you drain the potatoes. Reheat, stirring in 1 tablespoon of chopped fresh thyme and salt and pepper to taste, then serve as a soup.

1 Place the potatoes, garlic and saffron in a large, heavy-based saucepan, add the stock and bring to the boil. Cover and simmer for 20 minutes, or until tender.

2 Meanwhile, brush the chicken breasts all over with half the olive oil and all of the lemon juice. Sprinkle with the fresh thyme and coriander and crushed coriander seeds. Heat a griddle pan, add the chicken and cook over a medium–high heat for 5 minutes on each side, or until the juices run clear when the meat is pierced with a skewer or the point of a knife. Alternatively, cook the chicken breasts under a preheated hot grill for 5 minutes on each side.

3 Drain the potatoes and return the contents of the sieve to the saucepan. Add the remaining olive oil and the milk, season to taste with salt and pepper and mash until smooth. Divide the saffron mash between 4 large, warmed serving plates, top with a piece of chicken and garnish with a few sprigs of fresh thyme. Serve.

minty lime chicken

serves 6

prep: 35 mins, plus 30 mins marinating

cook: 20 mins

These tasty, tangy lime and honey-coated chicken pieces have a matching sauce or dip based on creamy natural yogurt. Served with a fresh, crisp salad they are perfect for a filling lunch or light supper.

INGREDIENTS

3 tbsp finely chopped fresh mint

4 tbsp clear honey

4 tbsp lime juice

salt and pepper

12 boneless chicken thighs

mixed salad, to serve

SAUCE

150 g/5½ oz low-fat natural thick yogurt

1 tbsp finely chopped fresh mint

2 tsp finely grated lime rind

NUTRITIONAL INFORMATION

Calories	.170
Protein	.23g
Carbohydrate	.12g
Sugars	.12g
Fat	.3g
Saturates	.2g

cook's tip

When grilling chicken pieces under the hot grill or over the barbecue, do not line the grill rack with foil as it may catch some fat, then catch fire.

1 Mix the mint, honey and lime juice in a large bowl and season to taste with salt and pepper. Use cocktail sticks to keep the chicken thighs in neat shapes and add the chicken to the marinade, turning to coat evenly.

2 Cover with clingfilm and leave the chicken to marinate in the refrigerator

for at least 30 minutes, longer if possible. Remove the chicken from the marinade and drain. Reserve the marinade.

3 Preheat the grill to medium. Place the chicken on a grill rack and cook under the hot grill for 15–18 minutes, or until the chicken is tender and the juices run clear when a skewer is

inserted into the thickest part of the meat. Turn the chicken frequently and baste with the marinade. Alternatively, cook over hot coals on a lit barbecue.

4 Meanwhile, mix all the sauce ingredients together in a bowl. Remove the cocktail sticks and serve the chicken with a salad and the sauce for dipping.

spicy tomato chicken

cook: 10 mins

prep: 10 mins, plus 30 mins soaking

serves 4

These low-fat, spicy skewers are cooked in a matter of minutes – assemble ahead of time and store in the refrigerator until you need them. They are also ideal cooked on the barbecue.

NUTRITIONAL INFORMATION

Calories	195
Protein	28g
Carbohydrate	12g
Sugars	11g
Fat	4g
Saturates	1g

INGREDIENTS

500 g/1 lb 2 oz skinless, boneless chicken breasts

3 tbsp tomato purée

2 tbsp clear honey

2 tbsp Worcestershire sauce

1 tbsp chopped fresh rosemary

250 g/9 oz cherry tomatoes

fresh rosemary sprigs, to garnish

freshly cooked couscous or rice, to serve

cook's tip

Couscous is made from semolina that has been made into separate grains. It usually just needs moistening or steaming before serving.

1 Using a sharp knife, cut the chicken into 2.5-cm/1-inch chunks and place in a bowl. Mix the tomato purée, honey, Worcestershire sauce and rosemary together in a separate bowl, then add to the chicken, stirring to coat evenly.

 Soak 8 wooden skewers in a bowl of cold water for 30 minutes to prevent them burning during cooking. Preheat the grill to medium. Thread the chicken pieces and cherry tomatoes alternately on to the skewers and place them on a grill rack.

3 Spoon over any remaining glaze and cook under the preheated hot grill for 8–10 minutes, turning occasionally, until the chicken is cooked through. Transfer to 4 large serving plates, garnish with a few sprigs of fresh rosemary and serve with freshly cooked couscous or rice.

pan-fried chicken & coriander

serves 4 **prep: 15 mins** **cook: 15 mins**

It is difficult to believe that the rich-tasting sauce coating this flavoursome chicken doesn't contain lashings of double cream. Nevertheless, this is a low-fat dish and all it needs as an accompaniment is a steamed green vegetable or a crisp salad.

INGREDIENTS

1 bunch of fresh coriander	2 tbsp reduced-fat single cream
1 tbsp sunflower or corn oil	175 ml/6 fl oz Chicken Stock
4 skinless, boneless chicken	(see page 11)
breasts, about 115 g/4 oz each,	2 tbsp lime juice
trimmed of all visible fat	2 garlic cloves, finely chopped
1 tsp cornflour	1 shallot, finely chopped
1 tbsp water	1 tomato, peeled, deseeded
85 ml/3 fl oz low-fat	and chopped
natural yogurt	salt and pepper

NUTRITIONAL INFORMATION

Calories	.200
Protein	.27g
Carbohydrate	.6g
Sugars	.3g
Fat	.8g
Saturates	.3g

variation

Instead of fresh coriander, try using fresh tarragon. As tarragon is strongly flavoured, only use a few stems, otherwise it may overpower the dish.

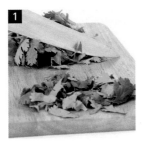

cook's tip

Wrap the chicken portions in pieces of foil to keep warm and to prevent them drying out after cooking. Before serving, remove from the foil and transfer to plates.

1 Reserve a few coriander sprigs for a garnish and roughly chop the remainder. Heat the sunflower oil in a heavy-based frying pan, add the chicken and cook over a medium heat for 5 minutes on each side, or until the juices run clear when the meat is pierced with a skewer or the point of a knife. Remove from the frying pan and keep warm.

2 Mix the cornflour and water until smooth. Stir in the yogurt and cream. Pour the Chicken Stock and lime juice into the frying pan and add the garlic and shallot. Reduce the heat and simmer for 1 minute. Stir the tomato into the yogurt mixture and stir the mixture into the frying pan. Season to taste with salt and pepper. Cook, stirring constantly, for 1–2 minutes, or until slightly thickened, but do not let the mixture boil. Stir in the chopped fresh coriander.

3 Place the chicken on a large serving plate, pour the sauce over it and garnish with the reserved coriander sprigs. Serve.

chicken with mustard

serves 4   **prep: 10 mins** (ㄴ   **cook: 20 mins** (⏲

The combination of chicken and a mustard and orange sauce is quite irresistible. Cooking the dish is simplicity itself – and, as an extra benefit, so is clearing up afterwards.

INGREDIENTS

1 tbsp sunflower or corn oil

4 skinless, boneless chicken breasts, about 140 g/5 oz each, all visible fat removed

salt and pepper

2 large oranges, peeled and cut into segments, juice reserved (see Cook's Tip)

2 tsp cornflour

150 ml/5 fl oz low-fat natural yogurt

1 tsp wholegrain mustard

fresh parsley sprigs, to garnish

NUTRITIONAL INFORMATION	
Calories	.267
Protein	.34g
Carbohydrate	.16g
Sugars	.12g
Fat	.8g
Saturates	.2g

variation

Omit the oranges and make the sauce with 2 tablespoons of lemon juice and 1 teaspoon of Dijon mustard instead of the wholegrain.

cook's tip

Use a sharp knife to peel the oranges and make sure that you remove all the pith. Hold the oranges over a bowl to catch the juices and cut down between the membranes to separate into segments.

1 Heat the oil in a large, heavy-based frying pan. Add the chicken breasts and cook over a medium–high heat for 5 minutes on each side, or until tender and the juices run clear when the meat is pierced with a skewer or the point of a knife. Season with a little salt and pepper, remove the chicken from the frying pan, cover with foil and keep warm.

2 Pour the orange juice into a small bowl and stir in the cornflour to make a smooth paste. Stir in the yogurt and mustard, then pour into the frying pan and bring to the boil over a low heat, stirring constantly.

3 Add the orange segments to the frying pan and season to taste with salt and pepper. Stir in any juices that have collected from the chicken. Spoon the sauce on to 4 large, warmed serving plates and top with the chicken. Garnish with parsley sprigs and serve immediately.

chicken fricassée

serves 4   **prep: 15 mins**   **cook: 35–40 mins**

While it is typically cooked in cream, the term fricassée merely denotes cooking the meat – or sometimes fish – in a white sauce, without browning it. Serve with plain boiled rice or new potatoes for a filling supper.

INGREDIENTS

1 tbsp plain flour	225 ml/8 fl oz Chicken Stock
salt and white pepper	(see page 11)
4 skinless, boneless chicken	2 carrots, diced
breasts, about 140 g/5 oz each,	2 celery sticks, diced
trimmed of all visible fat and	225 g/8 oz frozen peas
cut into 2-cm/¾-inch cubes	1 yellow pepper, deseeded and diced
1 tbsp sunflower or corn oil	115 g/4 oz button mushrooms, sliced
8 baby onions	125 ml/4 fl oz low-fat natural yogurt
2 garlic cloves, crushed	3 tbsp chopped fresh parsley

NUTRITIONAL INFORMATION

Calories	.287
Protein	.37g
Carbohydrate	.17g
Sugars	.8g
Fat	.8g
Saturates	.2g

variation

You can substitute skimmed milk for the yogurt and add extra flavour with 1 teaspoon of lemon juice and a pinch of freshly grated nutmeg in Step 3.

cook's tip

When slicing or dicing pepper halves, place them on a chopping board, shiny side downwards, to prevent the knife from slipping.

1 Spread out the flour on a dish and season with salt and pepper. Add the chicken and, using your hands, coat in the flour. Heat the oil in a heavy-based saucepan. Add the onions and garlic and cook over a low heat, stirring occasionally, for 5 minutes. Add the chicken and cook, stirring, for 10 minutes, or until just beginning to colour.

2 Gradually stir in the Chicken Stock, then add the carrots, celery and peas. Bring to the boil, then reduce the heat, cover and simmer for 5 minutes. Add the pepper and mushrooms, cover and simmer for a further 10 minutes.

3 Stir in the yogurt and chopped parsley and season to taste with salt and pepper. Cook for 1–2 minutes, or until heated through, then transfer to 4 large, warmed serving plates and serve.

roast turkey with cider sauce

serves 8

prep: 15 mins, ↺
plus 10 mins cooling

cook: 1 hr 40 mins ⏲

Most supermarkets sell boneless turkey breast roast. There is no waste, so it is an economical choice when entertaining and it fits into the oven more easily than a whole bird. Rolling the turkey around the stuffing helps to keep it moist during cooking.

INGREDIENTS

1 kg/2 lb 4 oz boneless turkey breast roast

salt and pepper

1 tbsp sunflower or corn oil

115 g/4 oz prunes, stoned and chopped

55 g/2 oz raisins

3 tbsp Chicken Stock (see page 11)

4 tbsp dry cider

1 tbsp chopped fresh parsley

STUFFING

25 g/1 oz butter

2 shallots, finely chopped

1 celery stick, finely chopped

1 cooking apple, peeled, cored and diced

SAUCE

1 shallot, very finely chopped

300 ml/10 fl oz dry cider

125 ml/4 fl oz Chicken Stock

1 tsp cider vinegar

NUTRITIONAL INFORMATION	
Calories	220
Protein	30g
Carbohydrate	13g
Sugars	13g
Fat	4g
Saturates	2g

variation

Use 1.3 kg/3 lb whole chicken instead. Fill the neck with stuffing and roast for 1½ hours. Roll the remaining stuffing into balls and bake for 15 minutes.

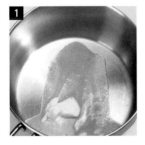

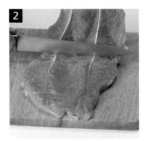

cook's tip

If you want to prepare part of this dish in advance, make the stuffing the day before and keep in the refrigerator until required.

1 Preheat the oven to 190°C/375°F/Gas Mark 5. To make the stuffing, melt the butter in a saucepan. Add the shallots and cook for 5 minutes. Add the celery and apple and cook for 5 minutes. Add the remaining stuffing ingredients, cover and simmer for 5 minutes, or until all the liquid has been absorbed. Transfer to a bowl and cool.

2 Place the turkey roast on a chopping board and slice almost completely through, from the thin side towards the thicker side. Open out, place between 2 sheets of clingfilm and flatten with a meat mallet or rolling pin to an even thickness. Season with salt. Spoon on the cooled stuffing, roll the roast around it and tie with kitchen string.

Heat the oil in a roasting tin over a medium heat, then add the roast and brown. Transfer to the preheated oven and roast for 1 hour 10 minutes, or until cooked through and the juices run clear when the meat is pierced with a skewer.

3 Remove the roast from the tin and cover with foil. To make the sauce, pour off any fat from the tin and set over a medium heat. Add the shallot and half the cider and cook for 1–2 minutes, scraping any sediment from the base of the tin. Add the remaining cider, stock and vinegar and cook for 10 minutes, or until reduced and thickened. Remove and discard the string from the turkey and cut into slices. Serve with the sauce.

vegetable & tofu stir-fry

serves 4　　　　　**prep: 10 mins,** ↺
plus 2 hrs marinating　　　　　**cook: 12 mins** ⏱

Tofu, also known as bean curd, is a low-fat source of high-quality protein for vegetarians. Although it is naturally bland, it absorbs the flavours of other ingredients, especially if it is marinated. Store tofu in the refrigerator, covered with cold water, for up to 3 days, changing the water daily. Drain and pat dry before use.

INGREDIENTS

225 g/8 oz firm tofu (drained weight),
cut into bite-sized pieces
1 tbsp groundnut or sunflower oil
2 spring onions, chopped
1 garlic clove, finely chopped
115 g/4 oz baby corn cobs, halved
115 g/4 oz mangetout
115 g/4 oz shiitake mushrooms,
thinly sliced
2 tbsp finely chopped fresh
coriander leaves

MARINADE
2 tbsp dark soy sauce
1 tbsp Chinese rice wine
2 tsp brown sugar
½ tsp Chinese five-spice powder
1 fresh red chilli, deseeded and
finely chopped
2 spring onions, finely chopped
1 tbsp grated fresh root ginger

NUTRITIONAL INFORMATION	
Calories	135
Protein	11g
Carbohydrate	7g
Sugars	5g
Fat	7g
Saturates	3g

variation

Substitute baby carrots, celery and courgettes, cut into batons, for the baby corn cobs and mangetout.

cook's tip

Always drain firm tofu, because it is packaged in water. Use a small, sharp knife for cutting the tofu – a blunt knife will squash it.

1 Place all the marinade ingredients in a large, shallow, non-metallic dish and stir to mix. Add the bite-sized chunks of tofu and turn them over carefully to coat thoroughly in the marinade. Cover the dish with clingfilm and leave the tofu in the refrigerator to marinate for 2 hours, turning the chunks over once or twice.

2 Drain the tofu and reserve the marinade. Heat the groundnut oil in a preheated wok or large frying pan. Add the tofu and stir-fry over a medium–high heat for 2–3 minutes, or until golden. Using a slotted spoon, remove the tofu from the wok and reserve. Add the spring onions and garlic and stir-fry for 2 minutes, then add the corn cobs and stir-fry for 1 minute. Add the mangetout and mushrooms and stir-fry for a further 2 minutes.

3 Return the tofu to the wok and add the marinade. Cook gently for 1–2 minutes, or until heated through. Sprinkle with the chopped fresh coriander and serve immediately.

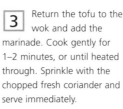

moroccan vegetable stew

serves 4 | **prep: 25 mins** | **cook: 45 mins**

This colourful selection of vegetables is simmered in a stock flavoured with lots of warming and aromatic spices.

INGREDIENTS

425 g/15 oz canned chickpeas

4 tomatoes, peeled and deseeded

700 ml/1¼ pints Vegetable Stock
(see page 11)

1 onion, peeled and sliced

2 carrots, peeled and sliced diagonally

1 tbsp chopped fresh coriander

salt

175 g/6 oz courgettes, sliced

1 small turnip, peeled and cubed

½ tsp ground turmeric

¼ tsp ground ginger

¼ tsp ground cinnamon

225 g/8 oz couscous

fresh coriander sprigs, to garnish

NUTRITIONAL INFORMATION	
Calories	.299
Protein	.13g
Carbohydrate	.56g
Sugars	.7g
Fat	.4g
Saturates	.0g

cook's tip

You can also cook the couscous by putting it into a large heatproof bowl and pouring over enough boiling water to cover. Leave to stand for 5–8 minutes, then fluff up with a fork and serve.

1 Drain the chickpeas, rinse under cold running water and reserve. Roughly chop the tomatoes and reserve half. Place the remainder in a blender or food processor and process until a smooth purée forms. Transfer to a large saucepan and add 400 ml/14 fl oz of the Vegetable Stock. Bring to the boil, then reduce the heat and add the onion, carrots, chopped fresh coriander and salt to taste. Simmer, stirring occasionally, for 10 minutes.

2 Stir in the courgettes, turnip, turmeric, ginger and cinnamon. Partially cover and simmer for a further 30 minutes. Stir in the reserved chickpeas and simmer for a few more minutes.

3 Meanwhile, bring the remaining Vegetable Stock to the boil in a heavy-based saucepan. Add a pinch of salt, then sprinkle in the couscous, stirring constantly. Remove the saucepan from the heat, cover with a tight-fitting lid and leave to stand for 5 minutes. Fluff up the couscous with a fork and transfer to 4 serving plates.

Top with the vegetables and their stock, garnish with a few sprigs of fresh coriander and serve immediately.

stuffed cabbage rolls

⏱ **cook: 1 hr 10 mins**   ⏱ **prep: 30 mins**   **serves 4**

Bathed in a sweet tomato sauce, these cabbage rolls are stuffed with a nutty filling of pearl barley and courgettes.

NUTRITIONAL INFORMATION	
Calories 224	
Protein 6g	
Carbohydrate 43g	
Sugars 19g	
Fat 5g	
Saturates 1g	

INGREDIENTS

8 large or 12 medium green
cabbage leaves
1 litre/1¾ pints water
100 g/3½ oz pearl barley
2 tbsp chopped fresh parsley
2 garlic cloves, roughly chopped
800 g/1 lb 12 oz canned chopped tomatoes
4 tbsp red wine vinegar
1 tbsp sunflower or corn oil, plus
extra for brushing
2 courgettes, diced
3 spring onions, sliced
salt and pepper
2 tbsp brown sugar

cook's tip

Substitute the pearl barley with long-grain rice. Cook the rice with half the parsley in a large saucepan of boiling water for 18–20 minutes in Step 1. Drain and proceed as in main recipe.

1 Preheat the oven to 190°C/375°F/Gas Mark 5. Cut out the stems from the cabbage leaves, then blanch the leaves in boiling water for 1 minute. Drain and spread out to dry. Bring the water to the boil in a saucepan. Add the barley and half the parsley. Reduce the heat, cover and cook for 45 minutes, until the liquid has been absorbed.

2 Meanwhile, put the garlic, 400 g/14 oz of the tomatoes and the vinegar in a blender or food processor and process until smooth. Transfer to a bowl and reserve. Heat the oil in a large frying pan. Add the courgettes and the remaining parsley and cook over a medium heat for 3 minutes. Add the spring onions and cook briefly, then

add the tomato mixture and cook for 10 minutes, or until thickened. Transfer to a bowl.

3 Add the cooked barley to the bowl, season to taste with salt and pepper and stir well. Lightly brush an ovenproof dish with oil. Place a spoonful of the barley mixture at the stem end of a cabbage leaf. Roll up, tucking in the

sides, and place, seam-side down, in the dish. Stuff and roll the remaining cabbage leaves in the same way, placing them in the dish in a single layer. Sprinkle the brown sugar over the rolls and pour the remaining tomatoes, with their can juice, on top. Cover with foil and bake in the oven for 30 minutes, or until tender. Serve straight from the dish.

lemony spaghetti

cook: 25 mins　　　　**prep: 10 mins**　　　　**serves 4**

variation

Replace the low-fat natural fromage frais with low-fat natural yogurt and add your favourite combination of vegetables, if you prefer.

Steaming vegetables helps to preserve their nutritional content, and allows them to retain their bright, natural colours and crunchy texture. This dish is best served immediately.

INGREDIENTS

225 g/8 oz celeriac

2 medium carrots

2 medium leeks

1 small red pepper

1 small yellow pepper

2 garlic cloves

1 tsp celery seeds

1 tbsp lemon juice

300 g/10½ oz dried spaghetti

celery leaves, chopped, to garnish

DRESSING

1 tsp finely grated lemon rind

1 tbsp lemon juice

4 tbsp low-fat natural fromage frais

salt and pepper

2 tbsp snipped fresh chives

cook's tip

Use a pair of kitchen scissors to snip chives. Cut the chives over a small bowl and add them at the very end to retain their delicate flavour.

1 To prepare the vegetables, peel the celeriac and carrots, then, using a sharp knife, cut into thin matchsticks and place in a large bowl. Trim and slice the leeks, rinse under cold running water to flush out any trapped dirt, then shred finely. Halve, deseed and slice the peppers and thinly slice the garlic. Add all the vegetables to the bowl with the celeriac and carrots. Add the celery seeds and lemon juice and toss until thoroughly mixed.

2 Cook the spaghetti in a large, heavy-based saucepan of boiling water according to the packet instructions, or until tender but still firm to the bite. Drain and keep warm.

3 Meanwhile, bring another large saucepan of water to the boil, place the vegetables in a steamer or meat sieve and place over the boiling water. Cover and steam for 6–7 minutes, or until tender. While the spaghetti and vegetables are cooking, mix all the ingredients for the dressing together. Transfer the spaghetti and vegetables to a warmed serving bowl or 4 warmed serving plates and mix with the dressing. Garnish with chopped celery leaves and serve immediately.

fish & shellfish

*The perfect choice for healthy eating, all fish and shellfish – even so-called oily fish –
are naturally low in fat. Nutritionists recommend that we should eat fish two or three times a
week, and the recipes featured in this chapter will make that both easy and pleasurable to do.
Fish and shellfish are among the most versatile of ingredients and go well with a wide range
of vegetables, herbs and spices, and with cheese, pasta and rice. The huge choice of fish
available today ensures that there is a dish to suit all tastes and budgets.*

*Recipes range from familiar favourites, such as Smoked Haddock Pie (see page 176)
and Mussels in White Wine (see page 198) to more unusual dishes, such as Cajun-spiced Fish
(see page 194) and Sea Trout in a Salt Crust (see page 195). There are fabulous fish stews, such
as Louisiana Gumbo (see page 184), hot and spicy dishes, such as Indian Chilli Fish
(see page 181), easy midweek suppers, such as Cod with Cheese & Tomatoes (see page 166),
and flamboyant combinations for entertaining, such as Bouillabaisse (see page 196).*

*In many of the recipes, there is no reason why you shouldn't substitute your own
favourite fish for the one suggested. If sole seems too extravagant, use plaice or brill. If you can't
find swordfish steaks, try the same recipe with the humble cod. If you are lucky enough to find
affordable fresh langoustines, use them in one of the prawn recipes. The happy fact is that,
whatever fish you choose, you will be cooking a delicious and low-fat dish.*

cod provençal

serves 4 **prep: 10 mins** ⏲ **cook: 15 mins** ⏱

Easy to prepare and easy to eat – that is the keynote to this tasty fish dish. As it is also packed with protein and vitamins and contains hardly any saturated fat, you could not make a better choice for a quick and healthy midweek supper.

INGREDIENTS

4 cod steaks, about 140 g/5 oz each
150 ml/5 fl oz Fish Stock
(see page 11)
1 bay leaf
6 black peppercorns
strip of thinly pared lemon rind
2 thin slices of onion

SAUCE
400 g/14 oz canned chopped tomatoes
1 garlic clove, very finely chopped
1 tbsp sun-dried tomato purée
1 tbsp capers, drained and rinsed
16 black olives, stoned
salt and pepper

TO GARNISH
fresh flat-leaved parsley sprigs
lemon wedges

NUTRITIONAL INFORMATION	
Calories	168
Protein	23g
Carbohydrate	4g
Sugars	3g
Fat	7g
Saturates	1g

variation

Add a dash of Pernod to the tomato sauce in Step 3 to give the dish a little extra flavour.

cook's tip

If you don't have any freshly made Fish Stock, you can use a mixture of equal parts dry white wine and water, which works just as well.

1 First, make the sauce. Place the chopped tomatoes, garlic, tomato purée, capers, olives and salt and pepper to taste in a large, heavy-based saucepan over a low heat. Heat gently, stirring occasionally.

2 Meanwhile, place the fish in a shallow, flameproof casserole in a single layer. Pour in the Fish Stock and add the bay leaf, peppercorns, lemon rind and onion slices. Bring to the boil, then reduce the heat to very low, cover and simmer gently for 10 minutes, or until the fish is opaque and flakes easily when tested with the point of a knife. Using a fish slice, transfer the cod to a serving plate and keep warm.

3 Sieve the fish stock into the sauce and stir over a medium heat until slightly reduced. Pour the sauce over the fish, then garnish with a few sprigs of fresh parsley and lemon wedges. Serve.

fragrant tuna steaks

cook: 10–15 mins   **prep: 15 mins**   **serves 4**

NUTRITIONAL INFORMATION

Calories	.239
Protein	.42g
Carbohydrate	.0.5g
Sugars	.0.1g
Fat	.8g
Saturates	.2g

variation

Fresh salmon steaks would work equally well for this dish and substitute the lime rind and juice for lemon.

Fresh tuna steaks are very meaty – they have a firm texture, yet the flesh is succulent. Steaks from the belly are best of all. Tuna is very rich in valuable Omega-3 oils.

INGREDIENTS

4 tuna steaks, about 175 g/6 oz each
½ tsp finely grated lime rind
1 garlic clove, crushed
2 tsp olive oil
1 tsp ground cumin
1 tsp ground coriander
pepper
1 tbsp lime juice
1 tbsp chopped fresh coriander,
to garnish

TO SERVE
avocado relish (see Cook's Tip)
tomato wedges
lime wedges

cook's tip

For the relish, peel and chop a small avocado. Mix in 1 tablespoon lime juice, 1 tablespoon chopped coriander, 1 chopped red onion and some chopped tomato. Season to taste.

1 Using a sharp knife, trim the skin from the tuna steaks, rinse under cold running water and pat dry with kitchen paper.

2 Mix the lime rind, garlic, olive oil, ground cumin, ground coriander and pepper together in a bowl to make a paste and spread thinly on both sides of the tuna.

3 Heat a non-stick ridged griddle pan until hot and press the tuna steaks into the pan to seal them. Reduce the heat and cook for 5 minutes. Turn the fish steaks over and cook for a further 4–5 minutes, or until the fish is cooked through. Remove the fish from the griddle pan and drain on kitchen paper. Transfer to a serving plate.

4 Sprinkle the lime juice and chopped fresh coriander over the fish. Serve with the avocado relish and tomato and lime wedges.

italian sardines

serves 4   **prep: 20 mins** ↺   **cook: 8–10 mins** ⏲

Although they can be awkward and time-consuming to deal with, fresh sardines are a real treat. They are best cooked very simply – even just gutted and grilled or barbecued. Here they are flavoured with garlic and lemon rind and served with bruschetta. They would go well with a tomato and onion salad.

INGREDIENTS

1 tbsp olive oil
4 garlic cloves
650 g/1 lb 7 oz fresh sardines, gutted
and scaled (see Cook's Tip)
grated rind of 2 lemons
2 tbsp chopped fresh
flat-leaved parsley
salt and pepper
tomato and onion salad, to serve

BRUSCHETTA

4 thick slices of ciabatta or
other rustic bread
2 garlic cloves, halved
2 large tomatoes, halved

NUTRITIONAL INFORMATION

Calories	.405
Protein	.38g
Carbohydrate	.23g
Sugars	.4g
Fat	.19g
Saturates	.5g

variation

A variety of toppings can be used for the bruschetta. Try grilled pepper with fresh basil. Replace the ciabatta with French bread slices.

cook's tip

Gutting sardines is easy. Slit open the belly and remove the insides. Rinse and dry. To scale, hold the fish by its tail under running water and run your hand along the body from tail to head.

1 Preheat the grill to medium. Heat the olive oil in a large, heavy-based frying pan. Add the garlic and cook over a low heat until softened. Meanwhile, for the bruschetta, place the bread under the preheated hot grill and toast lightly on both sides. Transfer to a heatproof plate and keep warm in a low oven until required.

2 Add the sardines to the frying pan and cook for 5 minutes, turning once. Sprinkle with the grated lemon rind and chopped fresh parsley and season to taste with salt and pepper.

3 To finish the bruschetta, rub 1 side of each slice of toast with the cut side of a garlic clove, then with the cut side of a tomato. Divide the bruschetta and sardines between 4 serving plates and serve immediately with a tomato and onion salad.

cod with cheese & tomatoes

serves 4

prep: 10 mins, plus 30 mins marinating

cook: 25 mins

Fish and cheese have a natural affinity, but recipes usually suggest adding creamy sauces with the result that the fat content begins to soar. Here, fish is oven-baked, topped with halloumi and grilled.

INGREDIENTS

4 cod or other firm white fish fillets, about 175 g/6 oz each

grated rind and juice of 1 orange

8 canned anchovy fillets, drained and patted dry

175 g/6 oz halloumi cheese

4 beef tomato slices

fresh parsley leaves, to garnish

NUTRITIONAL INFORMATION	
Calories	159
Protein	19g
Carbohydrate	6g
Sugars	6g
Fat	7g
Saturates	4g

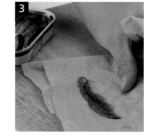

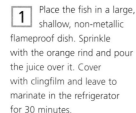

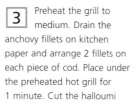

cook's tip

Citrus juices will begin to 'cure' fish after 1 hour, so make sure that you don't leave the fish to marinate for too long.

1 Place the fish in a large, shallow, non-metallic flameproof dish. Sprinkle with the orange rind and pour the juice over it. Cover with clingfilm and leave to marinate in the refrigerator for 30 minutes.

2 Preheat the oven to 180°C/350°F/Gas Mark 4. Remove the clingfilm

and re-cover the dish with foil. Bake in the preheated oven for 15–20 minutes, or until the flesh flakes easily.

3 Preheat the grill to medium. Drain the anchovy fillets on kitchen paper and arrange 2 fillets on each piece of cod. Place under the preheated hot grill for 1 minute. Cut the halloumi

cheese into 4 slices and place 1 slice on top of each cod fillet. Top with the tomato slices and return to the grill for a further 1–2 minutes, or until the cheese has charred slightly and the tomato is beginning to soften. Transfer to a serving plate, garnish with a few fresh parsley leaves and serve immediately.

monkfish with coconut

cook: 20–25 mins

prep: 30 mins, plus 4 hrs marinating

serves 4

These are tasty kebabs with a mild marinade. Allow the skewers to marinate for at least 1 hour before cooking. Serve with a crisp salad or freshly cooked rice as part of a buffet or summer barbecue.

NUTRITIONAL INFORMATION	
Calories	193
Protein	39g
Carbohydrate	2g
Sugars	2g
Fat	3g
Saturates	1g

INGREDIENTS

450 g/1 lb monkfish tails

225 g/8 oz raw peeled prawns

desiccated coconut, toasted,
to garnish (optional)

MARINADE

1 tsp sunflower oil

½ small onion, finely grated

1 tsp fresh root ginger, grated

150 ml/5 fl oz canned coconut milk

2 tbsp chopped fresh coriander

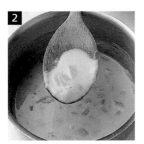

cook's tip

If using wooden skewers, remember to soak them in a bowl of cold water for 30 minutes to prevent them burning during cooking.

1 To make the marinade, heat the sunflower oil in a large, heavy-based saucepan and fry the onion and ginger for 5 minutes, until just softened but not browned.

2 Add the coconut milk to the saucepan and bring to the boil. Boil rapidly for 5 minutes or until reduced to the consistency of single cream. Remove from the heat and leave to cool completely.

3 When cooled, stir the coriander into the coconut milk and pour into a shallow dish. Cut the fish into bite-sized chunks and stir into the coconut mixture together with the prawns. Cover and leave to marinate in the refrigerator for 1–4 hours.

4 Preheat the grill to medium. Thread the fish and prawns on to metal or presoaked wooden skewers and discard any remaining marinade. Cook the skewers under the preheated hot grill for 10–15 minutes, turning frequently. Alternatively, cook over hot coals on a preheated barbecue. Garnish with toasted desiccated coconut and serve.

yucatan fish

serves 4　　　**prep: 10 mins,**　　　**cook: 40 mins**
plus 30 mins marinating

*Plenty of fresh herbs, onion, green pepper and pumpkin seeds
are used to flavour this delicious baked fish dish, which is first
marinated in a little lime juice. Serve straight from the oven with
freshly cooked rice or steamed broccoli, if you like.*

INGREDIENTS

4 cod cutlets or steaks or hake cutlets,	1 tbsp chopped fresh coriander
about 175 g/6 oz each	or parsley
2 tbsp lime juice	1 tbsp chopped fresh mixed herbs
salt and pepper	55 g/2 oz button mushrooms,
1 green pepper	thinly sliced
1 tbsp olive oil	2–3 tbsp fresh orange juice or white wine
1 onion, chopped finely	
1–2 garlic cloves, crushed	TO GARNISH
40 g/1½ oz green pumpkin seeds	lime wedges
grated rind of ½ lime	fresh mixed herbs

NUTRITIONAL INFORMATION

Calories	.248
Protein	.33g
Carbohydrate	.3g
Sugars	.2g
Fat	.11g
Saturates	.1g

variation

Replace the cod cutlets or steaks with
a whole cleaned fish, such as red
mullet or rainbow trout.

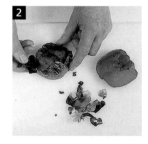

cook's tip

When marinating fish in lime
juice, do not leave for longer
than the recipe states, otherwise the lime juice will begin
to preserve it.

 1 Wipe the fish with
kitchen paper, place in
a shallow ovenproof dish and
pour over the lime juice. Turn
the fish in the juice, season
with salt and pepper, cover
and leave to marinate in the
refrigerator for 15–30 minutes.

2 Preheat the grill to
medium. Halve the
pepper, remove the seeds and

place under the preheated hot
grill, skin-side upwards, until
the skin burns and splits. Leave
to cool slightly, then peel off
the skin and chop the flesh.

3 Preheat the oven to
180°C/350°F/Gas
Mark 4. Heat the olive oil in a
frying pan and fry the onion,
garlic, pepper and pumpkin
seeds until the onion is soft.

4 Stir in the lime rind,
chopped coriander or
parsley, mixed herbs,
mushrooms and salt and
pepper to taste, then spoon
over the fish. Spoon or pour
the orange juice or wine over
the fish, cover and cook in
the preheated oven for
30 minutes, or until the fish is
just tender. Garnish with lime
wedges and herbs and serve.

smoked haddock pie

serves 4   prep: 15 mins   cook: 50–55 mins

Real comfort food, fish pie is a family favourite and there is no reason to go without. Using skimmed milk and reduced-fat cheese won't affect the flavour adversely, but will ensure a healthier meal.

INGREDIENTS

750 g/1 lb 10 oz floury potatoes, cut into chunks

salt and pepper

450 g/1 lb smoked haddock fillets

600 ml/1 pint skimmed milk

4 juniper berries

4 black peppercorns

1 bay leaf

2 tbsp plain flour

325 g/11½ oz canned sweetcorn, drained

25 g/1 oz butter

55 g/2 oz reduced-fat Cheddar cheese, grated

fresh flat-leaved parsley sprigs, to garnish

NUTRITIONAL INFORMATION

Calories 478

Protein 38g

Carbohydrate 69g

Sugars 17g

Fat 7g

Saturates 4g

variation

For a slightly different fish pie, try substituting smoked cod, whiting or coley for the smoked haddock.

cook's tip

For the healthiest choice, look for naturally pale smoked haddock, rather than the bright yellow dyed fish, and canned sweetcorn with no added salt or sugar.

1 Preheat the oven to 200°C/400°F/Gas Mark 6. Cook the potatoes in a large saucepan of lightly salted boiling water for 20 minutes, or until tender. Meanwhile, place the fish in a large frying pan, pour in the milk and add the juniper berries, peppercorns and bay leaf. Cover and simmer over a low heat for 10 minutes, or until the flesh flakes easily. Transfer the fish to a chopping board. Sieve the milk and reserve. When the fish is cool enough to handle, remove and discard the skin and any small remaining bones. Flake the flesh and place in a bowl.

2 Place the flour in a saucepan and gradually whisk in 400 ml/14 fl oz of the reserved milk, setting the rest aside. Bring to the boil over a low heat, stirring, then simmer for 1 minute. Season to taste with salt and pepper. Add the sauce to the fish with the sweetcorn, then spoon into an ovenproof dish.

3 When the potatoes are tender, drain well, then mash with the butter and remaining milk. Spoon the mash over the fish, spreading it out to cover. Sprinkle the cheese on top and bake in the preheated oven for 25–30 minutes, or until golden. Serve immediately, garnished with parsley sprigs.

fish & yogurt quenelles

cook: 15 mins

prep: 15 mins, plus 30 mins chilling

serves 4

NUTRITIONAL INFORMATION	
Calories	.228
Protein	.39g
Carbohydrate	.14g
Sugars	.7g
Fat	.2g
Saturates	.2g

These delicious quenelles, made from a thick purée of fish and yogurt, can be prepared well in advance and stored in the refrigerator before poaching.

INGREDIENTS

750 g/1 lb 10 oz white fish fillets, such as cod, coley or whiting, skinned

2 small egg whites

½ tsp ground coriander

1 tsp ground mace

salt and pepper

150 ml/5 fl oz low-fat natural yogurt

1 small onion, sliced

freshly cooked rice, to serve

SAUCE

1 bunch of watercress, trimmed

300 ml/10 fl oz Chicken Stock (see page 11)

2 tbsp cornflour

150 ml/5 fl oz low-fat natural yogurt

2 tbsp low-fat crème fraîche

variation

Replace the cod fillets with salmon. Add grated lemon rind and chopped fresh dill to the processor with the spices, then proceed as in main recipe.

cook's tip

When poaching the quenelles, make sure that the water is just gently bubbling, otherwise the quenelles will break up.

1 Cut the fish into pieces, place it in a food processor and process for 30 seconds. Add the egg whites and process for a further 30 seconds, or until the mixture forms a stiff paste. Add the ground coriander, mace, salt and pepper and yogurt and process until smooth. Cover and chill in the refrigerator for 30 minutes.

2 Spoon the mixture into a piping bag and pipe into sausage shapes 10 cm/ 4 inches long. Alternatively, take rounded dessertspoons of the mixture and form into ovals, using 2 spoons.

3 Bring about 5 cm/ 2 inches of water to the boil in a frying pan and add the onion for flavouring. Lower the quenelles into the water, using a fish slice or spoon. Cover, keep the water at a gentle boil and poach the quenelles for 8 minutes, turning them once. Remove with a slotted spoon and drain.

4 To make the sauce, roughly chop the watercress, reserving a few sprigs for garnish, then place the remainder in a food processor, add the Chicken Stock and process until well blended. Pour into a small saucepan. Stir the cornflour into the yogurt and pour the mixture into the saucepan. Bring to the boil, stirring. Stir in the crème fraîche, season to taste and remove from the heat. Garnish with the reserved watercress and serve with rice.

kedgeree

serves 4

prep: 15 mins, plus ⏳
10 mins cooling

cook: 40 mins ⏲

Derived from an Indian dish of rice, onions, lentils and eggs, kedgeree dates from the days of the British Raj. Fish was added and kedgeree became a staple for leisurely colonial breakfasts.

INGREDIENTS

225 g/8 oz haddock fillet

225 g/8 oz smoked haddock fillet

1 tbsp sunflower or corn oil

1 onion, chopped

½ tsp ground turmeric

½ tsp ground cumin

½ tsp chilli powder

¼ tsp ground ginger

225 g/8 oz long-grain rice

salt and pepper

TO GARNISH

1 hard-boiled egg

2 tbsp chopped fresh parsley

NUTRITIONAL INFORMATION	
Calories	340
Protein	27g
Carbohydrate	47g
Sugars	1g
Fat	5g
Saturates	1g

variation

Traditionally, 150 ml/5 fl oz single or soured cream is folded in with the fish. An alternative would be to use the same quantity of low-fat natural yogurt.

1 Place the haddock fillets in a large, heavy-based frying pan. Pour in enough water to cover and poach gently over a low heat for 10–15 minutes, or until the flesh flakes easily. Remove the fish with a fish slice and leave to cool. Sieve the cooking liquid into a measuring jug and make up to 600 ml/1 pint, if necessary.

2 Heat the oil in a flameproof casserole. Add the onion and cook over a low heat for 3 minutes, or until soft. Stir in the spices, then the rice, and cook, stirring, until well coated. Stir in the reserved cooking liquid. Bring to the boil, cover and cook over a low heat for 20 minutes, or until all the liquid has been absorbed and the rice is tender.

3 Meanwhile, skin the fish and remove any remaining bones, then flake the flesh. Fold the fish into the rice, season to taste with salt and pepper and transfer to a large, warmed serving dish. Shell the hard-boiled egg and cut into quarters, then use to garnish the kedgeree. Sprinkle with chopped fresh parsley and serve immediately.

indian chilli fish

cook: 10–20 mins **prep: 10 mins, plus 30 mins marinating** **serves 4**

The lime juice in this Indian-style recipe helps protect the delicate flesh of the fish from the fierce heat of the grill during cooking. However, keep an eye open and lower the heat if it seems too dry.

NUTRITIONAL INFORMATION	
Calories	144
Protein	21g
Carbohydrate	3g
Sugars	3g
Fat	5g
Saturates	1g

INGREDIENTS

1-cm/½-inch piece fresh root ginger

4 plaice fillets, about 115 g/4 oz each

1 tbsp groundnut or sunflower oil

1 tbsp chopped fresh coriander

2 tbsp lime juice

300 ml/10 fl oz water

2 tbsp tomato purée

1 tbsp chilli sauce

1 tbsp white wine vinegar

1 tsp muscovado sugar

fresh coriander sprigs, to garnish

lime wedges, to serve

variation

This sauce is delicious with prawns. Add 450 g/1 lb cooked, peeled prawns to the sauce to heat through during the last 2–3 minutes of cooking.

1 Grate the ginger and set aside. Place the fish in a shallow, non-metallic dish. Pour in the groundnut oil, chopped coriander and lime juice and turn the fish to coat well. Cover with clingfilm and leave to marinate in the refrigerator for 30 minutes.

2 Preheat the grill to medium. Place the water, tomato purée, chilli sauce, vinegar, grated ginger and sugar in a small saucepan. Bring to the boil over a low heat, stirring. Simmer, stirring occasionally, for 5–8 minutes, or until thickened.

3 Meanwhile, remove the fish from the marinade and cook under the preheated hot grill for 5–8 minutes, or until the flesh is opaque and flakes easily. Transfer to 4 serving plates and spoon over the sauce. Garnish with coriander sprigs and serve with lime wedges.

sole paupiettes

serves 4   **prep: 10 mins** ⏲   **cook: 45 mins** ⏲

This delicate dish of sole fillets rolled up with spinach and prawns, then served in a creamy ginger sauce will be an instant favourite with both family and friends.

INGREDIENTS

125 g/4½ oz fresh young spinach leaves	2 thin slices fresh root ginger, chopped
2 Dover soles or lemon soles, filleted	150 ml/5 fl oz Fish Stock (see page 11)
salt and pepper	or water
125 g/4½ oz cooked, peeled prawns,	2 tsp cornflour
thawed if frozen	4 tbsp single cream
2 tsp sunflower oil	6 tbsp low-fat natural yogurt
2–4 spring onions, finely sliced	whole cooked prawns, to garnish

NUTRITIONAL INFORMATION

Calories 253

Protein 24g

Carbohydrate 9g

Sugars 7g

Fat 14g

Saturates 2g

variation

Replace the Dover sole with lemon sole fillets or plaice fillets and substitute twists of lemon for the cooked prawns.

cook's tip

If using frozen prawns, make sure that they are completely thawed out before cooking. Keep the prawns covered in the refrigerator until ready to use and always use on the same day as thawed.

1 Trim the stalks from the spinach and discard. Rinse the leaves under cold running water and pat dry on kitchen paper. Season the fish with salt and pepper, then divide the spinach among the seasoned fish fillets, laying the leaves on the skin side. Divide half the prawns among them. Roll up the fillets from head to tail and secure with wooden cocktail sticks. Arrange the rolls on a plate in the base of a large bamboo steamer.

2 Stand a low metal trivet in the wok and add enough water to come almost to the top of it. Bring to the boil. Place the bamboo steamer on the trivet, cover with the steamer lid, then the wok lid, or cover with a domed piece of foil. Steam gently for 30 minutes, or until the fish is tender and cooked through.

3 Remove the fish rolls and keep warm. Empty the wok and wipe dry with kitchen paper. Heat the oil in the wok until hot. Add the spring onions and ginger and stir-fry for 1–2 minutes.

4 Add the Fish Stock to the wok and bring to the boil. Blend the cornflour with the cream. Add the yogurt and remaining prawns to the wok and heat until boiling. Add a little sauce to the blended cream and return it all to the wok. Heat until thickened. Season to taste. Serve the paupiettes with the sauce and garnished with whole prawns.

bouillabaisse

serves 8   **prep: 30 mins, plus 30 mins marinating**   **cook: 20 mins**

This is probably the most famous fish stew in the world and just about every French village on the Mediterranean coastline has its own particular version. A good-quality fish stock is absolutely essential. Serve with plenty of French bread.

NUTRITIONAL INFORMATION

Calories	.359
Protein	.54g
Carbohydrate	.7g
Sugars	.2g
Fat	.13g
Saturates	.1g

INGREDIENTS

1.25 kg/2 lb 12 oz sea bass, filleted, skinned and cut into bite-sized pieces

1.25 kg/2 lb 12 oz redfish, filleted, skinned and cut into bite-sized pieces

3 tbsp extra virgin olive oil

grated rind of 1 orange

1 garlic clove, finely chopped

pinch of saffron threads

2 tbsp pastis

450 g/1 lb live mussels

1 large cooked crab

1 small fennel bulb, finely chopped

2 celery sticks, finely chopped

1 onion, finely chopped

1.2 litres/2 pints Fish Stock (see page 11)

225 g/8 oz small new potatoes

225 g/8 oz tomatoes, peeled, deseeded and chopped

450 g/1 lb large raw prawns

salt and pepper

variation

Replace the sea bass with whiting and substitute clams for the mussels. You could also add cooked, peeled prawns and garnish with whole cooked ones.

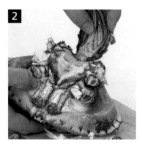

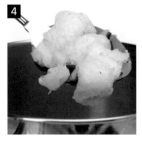

cook's tip

Redfish or Norwegian haddock is related to the scorpion fish. It is a traditional ingredient in bouillabaisse, but if you cannot find it, use red mullet instead.

1 Place the fish pieces in a large bowl and add 2 tablespoons of the olive oil, the orange rind, garlic, saffron and pastis. Turn the fish pieces to coat well, cover and leave in the refrigerator to marinate for 30 minutes.

2 Meanwhile, clean the mussels by scrubbing or scraping the shells and pulling off any beards that are attached to them. Remove the meat from the cooked crab and chop. Reserve.

3 Heat the remaining olive oil in a large flameproof casserole. Add the fennel, celery and onion and cook over a low heat, stirring occasionally, for 5 minutes, or until softened. Add the Fish Stock and bring to the boil. Add the new potatoes and tomatoes and cook over a medium heat for 7 minutes.

4 Reduce the heat and add the fish, beginning with the thickest chunks. Discard any mussels that do not close when sharply tapped with the back of a knife and add the remainder to the stew.

Add the prawns and pieces of crab and simmer until the fish is opaque, the mussels have opened again and the prawns have changed colour. Discard any mussels that remain closed. Season the bouillabaisse to taste with salt and pepper and serve immediately.

rigatoni with squid

serves 4   **prep: 10 mins** ⟲   **cook: 50–55 mins** ⟳

This delicious combination of pasta and squid is excellent for a light summer supper. If time is limited, use fresh pasta, as it takes less time to cook than dried. Farfalle and penne would also work well.

INGREDIENTS

1 red pepper	400 g/14 oz canned chopped tomatoes
1 yellow pepper	½–1 tsp chilli powder
1 tbsp sunflower or corn oil	250 g/9 oz dried rigatoni
350 g/12 oz prepared squid rings	2 tbsp chopped fresh basil
1 onion, chopped	salt and pepper
1 garlic clove, finely chopped	

NUTRITIONAL INFORMATION	
Calories	349
Protein	23g
Carbohydrate	56g
Sugars	10g
Fat	5g
Saturates	0g

variation

Use fresh tomatoes instead of canned when they are in season. Peel, deseed and chop 750 g/1 lb 10 oz tomatoes and add them in Step 2.

cook's tip

The trick with squid is to cook it very rapidly. It is only tough and rubbery when it is over-cooked. If stir-frying, cook the squid for 2 minutes, or until the rings are opaque.

1 Preheat the grill to medium. Place the peppers on a baking sheet and roast under the grill, turning frequently, for 15 minutes, or until charred and beginning to blacken. Remove with tongs, place in a polythene bag and seal the top. When the peppers are cool enough to handle, rub off the skins, deseed and chop the flesh.

2 Heat the oil in a heavy-based frying pan. Add the squid rings and stir-fry for 1–2 minutes, or until opaque. Remove the squid and reserve. Add the onion and garlic and cook for 5 minutes, or until softened. Add the tomatoes and peppers and chilli powder to taste, reduce the heat and simmer for 20–25 minutes, or until thickened.

3 Meanwhile, cook the pasta in a saucepan of lightly salted water for 8–10 minutes, or until tender but still firm to the bite. Just before serving, stir the squid rings and basil into the sauce and season to taste with salt and pepper. Heat through for 2–3 minutes. Drain the pasta, transfer to a serving dish and toss with the sauce. Serve.

warm currants in cassis

serves 4 **prep: 10 mins** ⏰ **cook: 10 mins** ⏱

Crème de cassis is a blackcurrant–based liqueur which comes from France and is an excellent flavouring for all types of fruit dishes. This dessert is the perfect way to end a meal, served with a little whipped cream or fat-free fromage frais.

INGREDIENTS

350 g/12 oz blackcurrants

225 g/8 oz redcurrants

4 tbsp caster sugar

grated rind and juice of 1 orange

2 tsp arrowroot

2 tbsp crème de cassis

whipped cream or fat-free

fromage frais

4 fresh mint sprigs, to decorate

NUTRITIONAL INFORMATION	
Calories 202	
Protein 2g	
Carbohydrate 35g	
Sugars 0g	
Fat 6g	
Saturates 4g	

variation

Fresh berries would also work well. Use the same amount of fresh blackberries and strawberries.

cook's tip

When stripping the currants from their stalks, just run the tines of a fork down the length of the stalk and the currants will come away very easily.

1 Using a fork, strip the blackcurrants and redcurrants from their stalks and place in a small, heavy-based saucepan.

2 Add the caster sugar and orange rind and juice, and heat gently, stirring, until the sugar has dissolved. Bring to the boil and simmer gently for 5 minutes.

3 Sieve the currants through a sieve and place in a bowl, then return the juice to the saucepan. Blend the arrowroot with a little water and mix into the juice in the saucepan. Boil the mixture until thickened.

4 Remove the saucepan from the heat and leave to cool slightly, then stir in the

crème de cassis. Transfer to 4 serving dishes, add a spoonful of whipped cream or fromage frais and decorate with fresh mint sprigs.

berry yogurt ice

serves 4   **prep: 15 mins,** ⏲   **cook: 5 mins** ⏱
plus 4 hrs freezing

This refreshing ice makes a wonderful summer dessert after a filling meal, as it is light and cooling without the richness – or fat – of ice cream. Serve with a selection of fresh summer berries.

INGREDIENTS

125 g/4½ oz raspberries
125 g/4½ oz blackberries
125 g/4½ oz strawberries
1 large egg

175 ml/6 fl oz Greek yogurt
125 ml/4 fl oz red wine
2¼ tsp powdered gelatine
fresh berries, to decorate

NUTRITIONAL INFORMATION	
Calories 118	
Protein 6g	
Carbohydrate 6g	
Sugars 6g	
Fat 6g	
Saturates 3g	

variation

Substitute 55 g/2 oz redcurrants for half the raspberries and 55 g/2 oz blackcurrants for half the blackberries.

cook's tip

Vegetarians can use a vegetarian gelatine, which is available in health food shops, to make this ice. Follow the instructions on the packet and proceed as in main recipe.

1 Place the raspberries, blackberries and strawberries in a blender or food processor and process until a smooth purée forms. Rub the purée through a sieve into a bowl to remove the seeds.

2 Break the egg and separate the yolk and white into separate bowls. Stir the egg yolk and yogurt into the berry purée and set the egg white aside.

3 Pour the wine into a heatproof bowl and sprinkle the gelatine on the surface. Leave to stand for 5 minutes to soften, then set the bowl over a saucepan of simmering water until the gelatine has dissolved. Pour the mixture into the berry purée in a steady stream, whisking constantly. Transfer the mixture to a freezerproof container and freeze for 2 hours, or until slushy.

4 Whisk the egg white in a spotlessly clean, greasefree bowl until very stiff. Remove the berry mixture from the freezer and fold in the egg white. Return to the freezer and freeze for 2 hours, or until firm. To serve, scoop the berry yogurt ice into glass dishes and decorate with fresh berries of your choice.

coffee ice cream

serves 6 | **prep: 1 hr, plus 6 hrs freezing** | **cook: 0 mins**

This Italian-style dessert tastes as if it is full of double cream. In fact, it isn't an ice cream at all. If you have an espresso machine, make the coffee in that, otherwise brew it double strength in a filter.

INGREDIENTS

25 g/1 oz plain chocolate

225 g/8 oz ricotta cheese

5 tbsp low-fat natural yogurt

85 g/3 oz caster sugar

175 ml/6 fl oz strong black coffee, cooled and chilled

½ tsp ground cinnamon

dash of vanilla essence

25 g/1 oz chocolate curls, to decorate

NUTRITIONAL INFORMATION

Calories	150
Protein	. . . . .6g
Carbohydrate	. . . . .21g
Sugars	. . . . .21g
Fat	. . . . .6g
Saturates	. . . . .4g

1 Grate the chocolate and reserve. Place the ricotta cheese, yogurt and sugar in a blender or food processor and process until a smooth purée forms. Transfer to a large bowl and beat in the coffee, cinnamon, vanilla essence and grated chocolate.

2 Spoon the mixture into a freezerproof container and freeze for 1½ hours, or until slushy. Remove from the freezer, turn into a bowl and beat. Return to the container and freeze for 1½ hours.

3 Repeat this beating and freezing process twice more before serving in scoops, decorated with chocolate curls. Alternatively, leave in the freezer until 15 minutes before serving, then transfer to the refrigerator to soften slightly before scooping.

variation

Omit the cinnamon and vanilla essence and substitute 40 g/1½ oz grated mint chocolate for the plain chocolate.

lemon granita

⏲ **cook: 5 mins**

⏱ **prep: 10 mins, plus 2 hrs freezing**

serves 4

Not quite a sorbet, but more than a cold drink, a granita is a deliciously refreshing way to cleanse the palate, and is an ideal dessert to serve after a spicy main course.

NUTRITIONAL INFORMATION	
Calories	115
Protein	0g
Carbohydrate	31g
Sugars	31g
Fat	0g
Saturates	0g

INGREDIENTS

450 ml/16 fl oz water

115 g/4 oz sugar

grated rind of 1 lemon

8 tbsp freshly squeezed lemon juice

lemon zest, to decorate

variation

You can substitute the grated rind of ½ orange and the same quantity of orange juice for the lemon rind and juice, if you like.

1 Place the water and sugar in a large, heavy-based saucepan and set over a low heat. Stir until the sugar has completely dissolved. Bring to the boil, then remove the saucepan from the heat and leave to cool.

2 Add the lemon rind and juice to the cooled syrup and stir well to combine, then pour the mixture into a large, shallow, freezerproof container and freeze for 2 hours, or until the lemon syrup is solid.

3 Plunge the base of the container into hot water for 30 seconds, then turn out the frozen syrup into a food processor. Process to small crystals, then spoon into serving bowls and decorate with lemon zest. Serve immediately.

peach sorbet

serves 4   **prep: 10 mins,** ⏲
plus 2 hrs freezing

cook: 0 mins ⏲

This is a cheating, but still effective way of making a luscious frozen dessert, full of intense fruit flavour. Serve in small dessert bowls as part of a dinner party menu.

INGREDIENTS

3 large, ripe peaches

1 tbsp lemon juice

1 tbsp clear honey

1 tsp Southern Comfort or

peach schnapps

mint leaves, to decorate

NUTRITIONAL INFORMATION

Calories	.57
Protein	.1g
Carbohydrate	.13g
Sugars	.13g
Fat	.0g
Saturates	.0g

variation

For a virtually instant strawberry sorbet, buy 500 g/1 lb 2 oz frozen strawberries and process as in main recipe with honey and Curaçao.

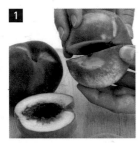

cook's tip

To peel a whole peach, make a tiny nick in the skin and place in a bowl. Cover with boiling water and leave for 15 seconds. Remove using a slotted spoon. Peel off the skin.

1 Using a sharp knife, cut the peaches in half, then remove and discard the stones. Place the peach halves in a bowl of boiling water and leave for 15 seconds. Remove from the bowl using a slotted spoon and peel off the skins. Cut the peaches into 2.5-cm/ 1-inch chunks and toss with the lemon juice. Spread the chunks out on a baking sheet,

cover with clingfilm and freeze for 2 hours, or until solid.

2 Remove the peaches from the freezer and place in a food processor. Pulse until granular, scraping down the sides from time to time.

3 Add the honey and Southern Comfort and process again until thoroughly

blended and fairly firm in consistency. Serve immediately, decorated with peach leaves or place in a freezerproof container and store in the freezer for up to 24 hours.

citrus meringue crush

⏲ **cook: 10 mins**

⏱ **prep: 1 hr, plus 2 hrs freezing**

serves 4

This is an excellent way to use up any leftover meringue shells and is easy and simple to prepare. Serve immediately with a spoonful of tangy kumquat sauce.

INGREDIENTS

8 ready-made meringue nests

300 ml/10 fl oz low-fat natural yogurt

½ tsp finely grated orange rind

½ tsp finely grated lemon rind

½ tsp finely grated lime rind

2 tbsp orange liqueur

2 tbsp lime juice

2 tbsp water

2–3 tsp caster sugar

1 tsp cornflour mixed with 1 tbsp water

SAUCE

55 g/2 oz kumquats

8 tbsp unsweetened orange juice

TO DECORATE

sliced kumquat

strips of lime rind

variation

You can replace the orange liqueur with the same amount of unsweetened orange juice, if you like.

cook's tip

Kumquats are now available from most large supermarkets. When buying, always choose ones that are unblemished. Before using, wash thoroughly under cold running water.

1 Place the meringues in a polythene bag and using a rolling pin, crush into small pieces. Place in a bowl. Stir in the yogurt, grated citrus rinds and the liqueur. Spoon the mixture into 4 mini-basins and freeze for 1½–2 hours, or until firm.

2 To make the sauce, using a sharp knife, thinly slice the kumquats and place them in a small saucepan with the fruit juices and water. Bring to the boil and simmer over a low heat for 3–4 minutes, or until the kumquats soften.

3 Sweeten with sugar to taste, stir in the cornflour mixture and cook, stirring, until thickened. Pour into a small bowl, cover the surface with clingfilm and leave to cool – the film will help prevent a skin forming. Leave to chill in the refrigerator until required.

4 To serve, dip the meringue basins in hot water for 5 seconds, or until they loosen, and turn on to 4 serving plates. Spoon over a little sauce, decorate with slices of kumquat and strips of lime rind and serve immediately.

chocolate cheese pots

serves 4   **prep: 10 mins, plus 30 mins chilling**   **cook: 0 mins**

These super-light desserts are just the thing if you have a craving for chocolate. They are delicious served on their own or with a selection of fresh fruit.

INGREDIENTS

300 ml/10 fl oz fat-free natural
fromage frais

150 ml/5 fl oz low-fat natural yogurt

25 g/1 oz icing sugar

4 tsp low-fat drinking
chocolate powder

4 tsp cocoa powder

1 tsp vanilla essence

2 tbsp dark rum (optional)

2 medium egg whites

4 chocolate shapes,
to decorate

TO SERVE

pieces of kiwi fruit, orange and banana

whole strawberries and raspberries

NUTRITIONAL INFORMATION

Calories	177
Protein	9g
Carbohydrate	18g
Sugars	17g
Fat	1g
Saturates	1g

variation

If liked, arrange 175 g/6 oz mixed summer berries in the bases before adding the mousse.

cook's tip

This mixture would make a good cheesecake filling. Make the base from crushed amaretti biscuits and egg white and set the filling with 2 teaspoons powdered gelatine dissolved in 2 tablespoons boiling water.

1 Mix the fromage frais and yogurt together in a bowl. Sift in the sugar, chocolate and cocoa powder and mix well. Add the vanilla essence and rum, if using.

2 Whisk the egg whites in a separate spotlessly clean, greasefree bowl until

stiff. Using a metal spoon, gently fold the egg whites into the chocolate mixture.

3 Spoon the fromage frais and chocolate mixture into 4 small china dessert pots or ramekin dishes and leave to chill in the refrigerator for 30 minutes.

4 Decorate each chocolate cheese pot with a chocolate shape and serve with an assortment of fresh fruit, such as pieces of kiwi fruit, orange and banana, and a few whole strawberries and raspberries.

indonesian black rice pudding

serves 4   **prep: 5 mins** ↺   **cook: 45 mins** ⏱

Also known as glutinous rice, even though it doesn't contain any gluten, sticky rice is available from Chinese supermarkets and may be black or white – the former is unpolished.

INGREDIENTS

115 g/4 oz black sticky rice

450 ml/16 fl oz water

55 g/2 oz dark brown sugar

55 g/2 oz caster sugar

300 ml/10 fl oz coconut milk, to serve

NUTRITIONAL INFORMATION

Calories	.228
Protein	.3g
Carbohydrate	.54g
Sugars	.33g
Fat	.1g
Saturates	.0g

variation

Add a small piece of bruised fresh root ginger when cooking the rice to add extra flavour. Remove and discard before serving.

1 Rinse the black sticky rice under cold running water, drain and place in a large, heavy-based saucepan. Add the water and bring to the boil, stirring constantly. Cover and simmer over a medium–low heat for 30 minutes.

2 Stir in both sugars and cook for a further 15 minutes. If necessary, add a little more water to prevent the rice from sticking.

3 Ladle the rice into 4 warmed bowls and serve immediately with the coconut milk. Alternatively, leave to cool completely and serve cold.

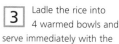

magic cheesecake

cook: 5 mins　　　　**prep: 15 mins, plus 1 hr chilling**　　　　**serves 6**

This superb dessert proves that you can have your cake and eat it too – or rather, you can indulge in a wonderful creamy and luxurious cheesecake and still stick to a healthy low-fat diet.

NUTRITIONAL INFORMATION

Calories 175

Protein 9g

Carbohydrate 22g

Sugars 12g

Fat 6g

Saturates 2g

INGREDIENTS

350 g/12 oz mixed fruits, such as star fruit, kiwi fruit, strawberries and kumquats

115 g/4 oz bran flakes, crushed

55 g/2 oz low-fat spread

6 tbsp apple juice

280 g/10 oz firm tofu (drained weight)

200 ml/7 fl oz low-fat natural yogurt

1 tbsp powdered gelatine

variation

If you like, try adding some finely grated lemon rind and the juice of 1 lemon to the yogurt and tofu mixture for extra flavour.

1 Prepare the fruits to lay on top of the cheesecake by washing, deseeding, peeling and slicing, as necessary, and reserve. Place the bran flakes in a polythene bag and crush them with a rolling pin.

2 Place the low-fat spread and 2 tablespoons of the apple juice in a saucepan over a very low heat and stir. When the spread has melted, stir in the bran flakes. Turn the mixture into a 23-cm/9-inch loose-based cake tin and press down with a wooden spoon to cover the base. Reserve.

3 Put the tofu and yogurt in a food processor and process until smooth, then transfer to a bowl. Pour the remaining apple juice into a heatproof bowl, sprinkle the gelatine over the surface and leave to stand for 5 minutes to soften. Set the bowl over a saucepan of simmering water for 5 minutes, or until the gelatine has dissolved, then pour into the tofu mixture in a steady stream, beating constantly. Spread over the base and chill until set.

4 Remove the cheesecake from the tin and place on a serving plate. Arrange the mixed fruits on top and serve.

almond cheesecakes

⏱ cook: 10 mins

🕒 prep: 15 mins,
plus 1 hr chilling

serves 4

NUTRITIONAL INFORMATION

Calories 361

Protein 16g

Carbohydrate 43g

Sugars 29g

Fat 15g

Saturates 4g

variation

Instead of the amaretti biscuits for the base, use crushed ginger biscuits. You can also substitute lemon for the lime.

These creamy cheese desserts are so delicious that it's hard to believe that they are low in fat. Served with plenty of fresh fruit, such as strawberries, blackberries and peaches, they are excellent for all special occasions.

INGREDIENTS

12 amaretti biscuits

1 medium egg white, lightly beaten

225 g/8 oz skimmed milk soft cheese

½ tsp almond essence

¼ tsp finely grated lime rind

25 g/1 oz ground almonds

25 g/1 oz caster sugar

55 g/2 oz sultanas

2 tsp powdered gelatine

2 tbsp boiling water

2 tbsp lime juice

TO DECORATE

25 g/1 oz toasted flaked almonds

strips of lime rind

cook's tip

When using baking paper, it is not necessary to oil the paper beforehand as the food very easily peels off after baking.

1 Preheat the oven to 180°C/350°F/Gas Mark 4. Place the biscuits in a large, clean polythene bag, seal the bag and using a rolling pin, crush them into small pieces.

2 Place the crumbs in a large bowl and bind together with the egg white.

3 Arrange 4 non-stick pastry rings or poached egg rings, 9 cm/3½ inches across, on a baking tray lined with baking paper. Divide the biscuit mixture into 4 equal portions and spoon it into the rings, pressing down well. Bake in the preheated oven for 10 minutes, or until crisp. Leave to cool in the rings.

4 Beat the soft cheese, almond essence, lime rind, ground almonds, sugar and sultanas together until well mixed. Dissolve the gelatine in the boiling water and stir in the lime juice. Fold into the cheese mixture and spoon over the biscuit bases. Smooth the tops and leave to chill in the refrigerator for

1 hour, or until set. Loosen the cheesecakes from the tins using a small palette knife or spatula and transfer to serving plates. Decorate with toasted flaked almonds and strips of lime rind and serve.

brown sugar pavlovas

serves 4 **prep: 25 mins, plus** ⏲ **1 hr cooling** **cook: 1 hr** ⏲

This simple combination of fudgy meringue topped with fat-free fromage frais and raspberries is the perfect finale to any meal.

INGREDIENTS

2 large egg whites

1 tsp cornflour

1 tsp raspberry vinegar

100 g/3½ oz light muscovado sugar, crushed free of lumps

2 tbsp redcurrant jelly

2 tbsp unsweetened orange juice

150 ml/5 fl oz fat-free natural fromage frais

175 g/6 oz raspberries, thawed if frozen

rose-scented geranium leaves, to decorate (optional)

NUTRITIONAL INFORMATION

Calories 155

Protein 51g

Carbohydrate 35g

Sugars 34g

Fat 0.4g

Saturates 2g

cook's tip

Make a large pavlova by forming the meringue into a round, measuring 18 cm/ 7 inches across, on a lined baking tray and bake in the preheated oven for 1 hour.

1 Preheat the oven to 150°C/300°F/Gas Mark 2. Line a large baking tray with baking paper. Whisk the egg whites in a spotlessly clean, greasefree bowl until very stiff and dry. Fold in the cornflour and vinegar. Gradually whisk in the sugar, a spoonful at a time, until the mixture is thick and glossy.

2 Divide the mixture into 4 portions and spoon on to the prepared baking sheet, spaced well apart. Smooth each portion into a round, 10 cm/4 inches across, and bake in the preheated oven for 40–45 minutes, or until lightly browned and crisp. Leave to cool on the baking tray until cold.

3 Place the redcurrant jelly and orange juice in a small saucepan and heat, stirring constantly, until melted. Remove the saucepan from the heat and leave to cool for 10 minutes. Using a palette knife, carefully remove each pavlova from the baking paper and transfer to a serving plate. Top with the fromage frais and the

raspberries. Glaze the fruit with the redcurrant jelly and decorate with the geranium leaves, if using.

paper-thin fruit pies

⏲ **cook: 15–20 mins**   ⏱ **prep: 20 mins**   **serves 4**

The extra-crisp pastry cases, filled with slices of fruit and glazed with apricot jam, are best served hot with low-fat custard.

NUTRITIONAL INFORMATION	
Calories	158
Protein	2g
Carbohydrate	14g
Sugars	0g
Fat	10g
Saturates	1g

INGREDIENTS

1 medium eating apple

1 medium ripe pear

2 tbsp lemon juice

55 g/2 oz low-fat spread

4 rectangular sheets of filo pastry, thawed if frozen

2 tbsp low-sugar apricot jam

1 tbsp unsweetened orange juice

1 tbsp finely chopped natural pistachio nuts, shelled

2 tsp icing sugar, for dusting

low-fat custard, to serve

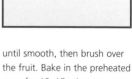

cook's tip

Other combinations of fresh fruit are equally delicious. Try peach and apricot, raspberry and apple, or mango and pineapple.

1 Preheat the oven to 200°C/400°F/Gas Mark 6. Core and thinly slice the apple and pear and toss them in the lemon juice. Gently melt the low-fat spread over a low heat.

2 Cut the sheets of pastry into 4 and cover with a clean, damp tea towel. Brush 4 non-stick Yorkshire pudding tins, measuring 10 cm/4 inch across, with a little of the low-fat spread.

3 Working on each pie separately, brush 4 sheets of pastry with low-fat spread. Press a small sheet of pastry into the base of one tin. Arrange the other sheets of pastry on top at slightly different angles. Repeat with the other sheets of pastry to make another 3 pies.

4 Arrange the apple and pear slices alternately in the centre of each pastry case and lightly crimp the edges of the pastry of each pie. Mix the jam and orange juice together until smooth, then brush over the fruit. Bake in the preheated oven for 12–15 minutes. Sprinkle with pistachio nuts, dust lightly with icing sugar and serve hot with custard.

carrot & ginger cake

⏱ **cook: 1 hr 15 mins**   ⏰ **prep: 15 mins, plus 1 hr 20 mins cooling**   **serves 10**

NUTRITIONAL INFORMATION	
Calories	.249
Protein	.7g
Carbohydrate	.46g
Sugars	.28g
Fat	6g
Saturates	.1g

variation

Instead of the topping, sprinkle a few pine kernels and crushed sugar lumps on top of the cake before baking.

This melt-in-the-mouth version of a favourite cake has a fraction of the fat of the traditional cake.

INGREDIENTS

butter, for greasing
225 g/8 oz plain flour
1 tsp baking powder
1 tsp bicarbonate of soda
2 tsp ground ginger
¼ tsp salt
175 g/6 oz light muscovado sugar
225 g/8 oz carrots, grated
2 pieces stem ginger in syrup, drained and chopped
25 g/1 oz fresh root ginger, grated
55 g/2 oz seedless raisins

2 medium eggs, beaten
3 tbsp corn oil
juice of 1 medium orange

FROSTING
225 g/8 oz low-fat soft cheese
4 tbsp icing sugar
1 tsp vanilla essence

TO DECORATE
stem ginger pieces
freshly grated root ginger

cook's tip

If you have a grater attachment on your food processor this will speed up the grating of the carrots. Remember to peel the carrots first.

1 Preheat the oven to 180°C/350°F/Gas Mark 4. Grease and line a 20-cm/8-inch round cake tin with baking paper.

2 Sift the flour, baking powder, bicarbonate of soda, ground ginger and salt into a bowl. Stir in the sugar, carrots, stem ginger, root ginger and raisins. Beat the

eggs, corn oil and orange juice together, then pour into the bowl. Mix well.

3 Spoon the mixture into the prepared tin and bake in the preheated oven for 1–1¼ hours, or until firm to the touch and a skewer inserted into the centre of the cake comes out clean. Leave to cool in the tin.

4 To make the frosting, place the soft cheese in a bowl and beat to soften. Sift in the icing sugar and add the vanilla essence. Mix well. Remove the cake from the tin and smooth the frosting over the top. Decorate the cake with pieces of stem ginger and a little grated fresh ginger, then serve.

apricot cake

serves 8   **prep: 20 mins, plus ◔ 40 mins cooling/chilling**   **cook: 1 hr 15 mins ⏲**

The moist, fruity layer of filling makes this lovely light cake a welcome treat with a cup of mid-morning coffee or as a dessert at the end of a midweek family supper.

INGREDIENTS

BASE	FILLING
200 g/7 oz plain flour, plus	125 g/4½ oz short-grain rice
extra for dusting	450 ml/16 fl oz skimmed milk
pinch of salt	85 g/3 oz caster sugar
55 g/2 oz caster sugar	grated rind and juice of ½ lemon
grated rind of ½ lemon	1 tbsp apricot jam
4 tbsp water	3 eggs, separated
90 g/3¼ oz unsalted butter, softened	800 g/1 lb 12 oz apricots, peeled,
	halved and stoned
	icing sugar, for dusting

NUTRITIONAL INFORMATION

Calories	.377
Protein	.9g
Carbohydrate	.63g
Sugars	.24g
Fat	.12g
Saturates	.7g

variation

For a change, replace the grated lemon rind and juice in the base and filling with the same amount of grated orange rind and juice.

cook's tip

To bake blind, prick the base all over with a fork, then line with baking paper. Partially fill with baking beans – either ceramic beans, or dried haricot beans kept specially for the purpose – and bake.

1 Preheat the oven to 200°C/400°F/Gas Mark 6. Sift the flour with a pinch of salt into a bowl and add the sugar, lemon rind, water and butter. Mix well, using an electric mixer or fork, until crumbly. Turn out on to a lightly floured work surface and knead lightly until smooth. Roll out and use to line the base and 3 cm/1¼ inches of

the sides of a 25-cm/10-inch springform cake tin. Chill in the refrigerator for 30 minutes, then bake blind in the oven for 10 minutes (see Cook's Tip).

2 Meanwhile, make the filling. Place the rice, milk, sugar and lemon rind in a small, heavy-based saucepan and bring to the boil. Reduce the heat and simmer for

30 minutes. Remove the saucepan from the heat, stir in the lemon juice and apricot jam and leave to cool.

3 Stir the egg yolks into the cooled rice mixture. Whisk the egg whites in a clean bowl until stiff, then fold gently into the rice mixture. Remove the cooked base from the oven, discard the baking

beans and lining paper and reduce the oven temperature to 180°C/350°F/Gas Mark 4. Arrange the apricot halves, flat side uppermost, over the base. Spoon the rice mixture over the top, spreading it out evenly. Bake for 45 minutes, or until a skewer inserted into the cake comes out clean. Cool on a wire rack and dust with icing sugar before serving.

strawberry roulade

serves 8   **prep: 30 mins**   **cook: 10 mins**

Serve this moist, light sponge rolled up with a tasty almond and strawberry fromage frais filling for a delicious teatime treat.

INGREDIENTS

3 large eggs

125 g/4½ oz caster sugar

125 g/4½ oz plain flour

1 tbsp hot water

FILLING

200 ml/7 fl oz low-fat fromage frais

1 tsp almond essence

225 g/8 oz small strawberries

15 g/½ oz flaked almonds, toasted

1 tsp icing sugar

variation

Replace the strawberries with other fresh fruit, such as mixed summer berries, a mix of red and green grapes or banana and kiwi fruit slices.

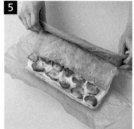

cook's tip

To prevent the sponge from breaking when you roll it up with the filling in place, manipulate it with the baking not your fingers, and work slowly and carefully.

1 Preheat the oven to 220°C/425°F/Gas Mark 7. Line a 35 x 25-cm/ 14 x 10-inch Swiss roll tin with baking paper. Place the eggs in a large bowl with the caster sugar, place over a saucepan of hot water and, using an electric whisk, whisk until pale and thick.

2 Remove the bowl from the saucepan. Sift in the flour and fold into the eggs with the hot water. Pour the mixture into the prepared tin and bake in the preheated oven for 8–10 minutes, or until golden and set.

3 Transfer the sponge to a sheet of baking paper. Peel off the lining paper and roll up the sponge tightly along with the baking paper. Wrap in a tea towel and cool.

4 Mix the fromage frais and almond essence together in a bowl. Reserving a few strawberries for the decoration, wash, hull and slice the rest. Leave the mixture to chill in the refrigerator until required.

5 Unroll the sponge, spread the fromage frais mixture over the sponge and sprinkle with strawberries. Roll the sponge up again and transfer to a serving plate. Sprinkle with almonds and lightly dust with icing sugar. Decorate with the reserved strawberries and serve.

fat-free marble cake

serves 8 **prep: 25 mins** ⏱ **cook: 45 mins** ⏱

For those of us who have a particularly sweet tooth, this beautifully light cake is too good to be true. The secret of its success lies in sifting the flour several times.

INGREDIENTS

sunflower oil, for brushing

100 g/3½ oz plain flour, sifted, plus extra for dusting

3 tbsp cocoa powder

225 g/8 oz caster sugar

pinch of salt

10 egg whites

1 tsp cream of tartar

½ tsp almond essence

½ tsp vanilla essence

icing sugar, for dusting

NUTRITIONAL INFORMATION

Calories 186

Protein 6g

Carbohydrate 40g

Sugars 30g

Fat 1g

Saturates 1g

cook's tip

When removing the baked cake from the oven, leave inverted in the tin on a wire rack, then tap the base gently all the way round. This will release it from the tin.

1 Preheat the oven to 180°C/350°F/Gas Mark 4. Oil and dust a 20-cm/8-inch deep cake tin. Sift 40 g/1½ oz of the flour with the cocoa powder and 2 tablespoons of the sugar into a bowl 4 times. Sift the remaining flour with 2 tablespoons of the sugar and the salt into a separate bowl 4 times.

2 Beat the egg whites in a spotlessly clean, greasefree bowl until soft peaks form. Add the cream of tartar and beat in the remaining caster sugar, 1 tablespoonful at a time, until the egg whites form stiff peaks. Whisk in the almond and vanilla essences. Divide the mixture in half. Fold the cocoa and flour mixture into

one half and the unflavoured flour into the other half. Spoon the cocoa flavoured mixture into the tin and top with the unflavoured mixture. Run a round-bladed knife through both mixtures to create a marbled effect.

3 Bake in the preheated oven for 45 minutes, or until a skewer inserted into the

centre of the cake comes out clean. Invert on to a wire rack to cool and dust with icing sugar before serving.

citrus honey cake

cook: 35 mins   **prep: 20 mins**   **serves 8**

This light-textured cake is drizzled with honey and lemon juice while it is still warm from the oven, giving it a rich and zesty flavour. Serve as a delicious dessert or a tasty afternoon snack.

NUTRITIONAL INFORMATION

Calories 158

Protein 4g

Carbohydrate 30g

Sugars 11g

Fat 3g

Saturates 1g

INGREDIENTS

sunflower or corn oil, for brushing

40 g/1½ oz reduced-fat sunflower margarine

4 tbsp clear honey

finely grated rind and juice of 1 lemon

150 ml/5 fl oz skimmed milk

140 g/5 oz plain flour

1½ tsp baking powder

½ teaspoon mixed spice

55 g/2 oz semolina

2 egg whites

2 tsp sesame seeds

cook's tip

Greek Hymettus honey, which has a distinctive aroma of thyme, would be especially delicious in this cake, as would the less expensive lemon blossom honey.

1 Preheat the oven to 200°C/400°F/Gas Mark 6. Lightly brush a 23-cm/9-inch round cake tin with oil and line the base with baking paper. Place the margarine and 3 tablespoons of the honey in a heavy-based saucepan and melt over a very low heat. Remove from the heat. Reserve 1 tablespoon of the lemon juice and stir the remainder into the honey mixture with the lemon rind and milk.

2 Sift the flour, baking powder and mixed spice into a bowl, then beat the mixture into the saucepan. Beat in the semolina. Whisk the egg whites in a separate spotlessly clean, greasefree bowl until soft peaks form, then gently fold them into the mixture. Spoon into the prepared tin and smooth the surface. Sprinkle the sesame seeds evenly on top.

3 Bake the cake in the preheated oven for 30 minutes, or until golden brown and springy to the touch. Mix the remaining honey and lemon juice in a small jug and pour it over the cake. Leave in the tin to cool before serving.

fruit loaf with apple spread

serves 4   **prep: 15 mins, plus 1 hr soaking/cooling**   **cook: 2 hrs**

This sweet, fruity loaf is ideal served for teatime or as a healthy snack at any time of the day. The fruit spread can be made quickly while the cake is baking in the oven.

INGREDIENTS

sunflower oil, for brushing

175 g/6 oz porridge oats

100 g/3½ oz light muscovado sugar

1 tsp ground cinnamon

125 g/4½ oz sultanas

175 g/6 oz seedless raisins

2 tbsp malt extract

300 ml/10 fl oz unsweetened apple juice

175 g/6 oz self-raising wholemeal flour

1½ tsp baking powder

SPREAD

225 g/8 oz strawberries, washed and hulled

2 eating apples, cored and chopped

300 ml/10 fl oz unsweetened apple juice

TO SERVE

whole strawberries

apple wedges

NUTRITIONAL INFORMATION

Calories	733
Protein	12g
Carbohydrate	17g
Sugars	110g
Fat	5g
Saturates	1g

variation

For a change, replace the strawberries with apple and blackberries or even strawberries and blackberries.

cook's tip

After preparing apples, sprinkle 1 tablespoon of lemon juice over them and mix until the apple pieces are coated as this prevents them discolouring.

1 Preheat the oven to 180°C/350°F/Gas Mark 4. Oil and line a 900-g/2-lb loaf tin with baking paper.

2 Place the porridge oats, sugar, cinnamon, sultanas, raisins and malt extract in a large bowl. Pour in the apple juice, stir well and leave to soak for 30 minutes.

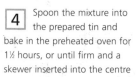

3 Sift in the flour and baking powder, adding any husks that remain in the sieve and fold in using a metal spoon.

4 Spoon the mixture into the prepared tin and bake in the preheated oven for 1½ hours, or until firm and a skewer inserted into the centre

comes out clean. Leave to cool in the tin for 10 minutes, then turn out on to a wire rack and leave to cool.

5 Meanwhile, make the fruit spread. Place the strawberries and apples in a saucepan and pour in the apple juice. Bring to the boil, cover and simmer for

30 minutes. Beat the sauce well and spoon into a clean, warmed jar. Leave to cool, then seal and label. Serve the loaf with 1–2 tablespoons of the spread and strawberries and apple wedges.

amaretti

makes about 40   **prep: 30 mins** ↻   **cook: 30 mins** ⏲

Traditionally, these moreish little Italian macaroons are made with apricot kernels, but almonds are used here. Serve amaretti with iced desserts or coffee at the end of a dinner party.

INGREDIENTS
150 g/5½ oz blanched almonds
150 g/5½ oz caster sugar
1 large egg white
icing sugar, for dusting

NUTRITIONAL INFORMATION	
Calories 38	
Protein 1g	
Carbohydrate 4g	
Sugars 0g	
Fat 2g	
Saturates 0g	

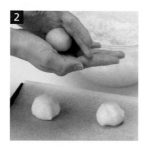

cook's tip

Commercially cooked amaretti obtain their distinctive flavour from a judicious mix of sweet and bitter almonds. Bitter almonds are not available to the home cook.

1 Preheat the oven to 120°C/250°F/Gas Mark ½. Place the almonds with the caster sugar in a mortar and crush with a pestle. Alternatively, finely chop the almonds and mix with the sugar in a bowl.

2 Lightly beat the egg white, then stir it into the almond mixture to form a firm dough. Line 2 baking sheets with baking paper and place walnut-sized portions of the dough, spaced well apart, on them. Dust with icing sugar.

3 Bake in the preheated oven for 30 minutes. Transfer to wire racks to cool completely, then serve.

fruity flapjacks

cook: 15–20 mins

prep: 10 mins, plus 10 mins cooling

makes 14

Great favourites with children for after-school snacks and popular with mums, too, as these tasty cereal bars are healthy, inexpensive and very easy to make.

NUTRITIONAL INFORMATION	
Calories	120
Protein	2g
Carbohydrate	19g
Sugars	0g
Fat	5g
Saturates	1g

INGREDIENTS

sunflower or corn oil, for brushing

140 g/5 oz rolled oats

115 g/4 oz demerara sugar

85 g/3 oz raisins

115 g/4 oz low-fat sunflower margarine, melted

variation

Substitute the same quantity of dried cranberries or blueberries for the raisins. These are now available in most supermarkets.

1 Preheat the oven to 190°C/375°F/Gas Mark 5. Lightly brush a 28 x 18-cm/11 x 7-inch shallow rectangular cake tin with oil.

2 Mix the oats, sugar and raisins and margarine together, stirring well.

3 Spoon the oat mixture into the prepared tin and press down firmly with the back of a spoon. Bake in the oven for 15–20 minutes, or until golden brown.

4 Using a sharp knife, score lines to mark out 14 bars, then leave to cool in the tin for 10 minutes. Transfer the bars to a wire rack to cool completely, then serve.

index